Agentic AI Integration: Leveraging MCP Servers for Intelligent Systems

Luca Randall

Preface

Welcome to *Agentic AI Integration: Leveraging MCP Servers for Intelligent Systems*. In these pages, we embark on a journey into the exciting world where artificial intelligence not only thinks but also interacts with its environment in smart, dynamic ways. If you've ever marveled at how a smartphone seamlessly connects to various apps, or wondered how your favorite smart home device communicates with multiple systems, you're already familiar with the power of standardized integration. Now, imagine applying that same principle to AI systems—this is where the Model Context Protocol, or MCP, comes in.

In our increasingly interconnected digital landscape, AI agents are evolving from isolated tools into true collaborators. They can access real-time information, learn from diverse data sources, and even perform tasks autonomously. However, unlocking their full potential has long been hindered by one major challenge: the need for each AI system to develop its own custom solutions to communicate with the outside world. This book is about solving that problem. MCP acts as a universal "language" that bridges AI models with the myriad tools and data sources they need to thrive, much like a common adapter that connects different devices effortlessly.

Throughout this book, we take a tutorial-driven approach to demystify MCP servers and explore their role in empowering intelligent systems. We'll begin by laying the groundwork—introducing the basic concepts of AI agents and the evolution of agentic systems. From there, we delve into the nuts and bolts of MCP: its architecture, communication protocols, and the ecosystem of servers that make these connections possible.

Think of this process like setting up a smart home. Initially, you have a collection of individual gadgets—each brilliant on its own—but without a central system to coordinate them, they can't truly work together. MCP is that central system for AI agents. It standardizes interactions, ensures seamless communication, and ultimately makes the whole experience more reliable, efficient, and secure.

I've always been fascinated by how technologies converge to simplify our lives. Whether it's the way USB-C cables now unify charging and data transfer across devices, or how modern smartphones integrate countless functionalities into one compact tool, the beauty lies in making complex systems work together effortlessly. With MCP, we see a similar promise for

AI: a future where these intelligent systems aren't siloed but are integrated into a unified, collaborative ecosystem.

This book is designed to be both an in-depth guide and a friendly companion for anyone looking to explore this transformative technology. As you turn these pages, you'll find that each chapter builds on the last, providing a logical progression from foundational concepts to advanced integration techniques and real-world applications. Our goal is not only to educate but also to inspire you to harness the power of agentic AI in your own projects, whether you're a developer, a business leader, or simply an enthusiast keen to understand the future of intelligent systems.

So, whether you're new to the concept of AI integration or you're looking to deepen your understanding of MCP servers, I invite you to dive in, explore, and imagine the possibilities. Together, we'll unlock the potential of AI that can truly connect, collaborate, and create a smarter digital world.

Welcome aboard!

TABLE OF CONTENTS

Introduction

Welcome to the beginning of an exciting journey into the world of intelligent systems, where AI agents don't just function—they collaborate, adapt, and transform the way we interact with technology. In this chapter, we'll explore the purpose of this book, give you a clear overview of what Agentic AI and the Model Context Protocol (MCP) are all about, and explain how this guide will equip you to integrate these groundbreaking concepts into your projects.

Purpose of the Book

At its core, this book is designed to bridge the gap between complex AI concepts and real-world applications. You may have heard about AI in the news or experienced its impact through smart devices in your home, but the real power of AI lies in its ability to interact with and leverage external data and tools. Historically, AI systems have been somewhat isolated—they operate based on the information they were trained on, often missing out on the dynamic, ever-changing landscape of real-world data.

Imagine trying to bake a cake with a cookbook that was written a decade ago. The ingredients, the techniques, even the recipes might have changed over time. Similarly, traditional AI models can struggle when they need to work with up-to-date information or interact with new tools. This is where Agentic AI and MCP come in. The purpose of this book is to demystify these concepts, showing you how to make your AI systems not only smarter but also more adaptable and integrated with the world around them.

Whether you're a developer looking to implement these technologies in a practical setting, a business leader aiming to harness AI for competitive advantage, or simply an enthusiast curious about the future of intelligent systems, this book will provide you with a comprehensive, tutorial-driven guide to understanding and applying these ideas.

Overview of Agentic AI and MCP

What is Agentic AI?

Agentic AI refers to artificial intelligence systems that are designed to act as independent agents—autonomous programs that can make decisions, learn from their experiences, and interact with various tools and data sources to accomplish tasks. Think of them as digital assistants on steroids. Unlike traditional AI, which often requires manual input for every action, agentic AI can operate in a self-directed manner. They learn from their environment, adapt to new information, and even collaborate with other agents to solve complex problems.

Imagine a team of highly skilled workers on a construction site. Each worker has a specific job, but they also communicate with each other, adjust their plans based on what others are doing, and work towards a common goal. Agentic AI operates in a similar fashion, dynamically interacting with both the data it receives and the tools it uses to achieve its objectives.

What is the Model Context Protocol (MCP)?

Now, consider how these intelligent agents can access the vast resources they need to function effectively. This is where the Model Context Protocol, or MCP, comes into play. MCP is like a universal adapter—a standard interface that connects AI models with external data sources and tools. Just as a USB-C cable can connect various devices regardless of the brand or model, MCP provides a common language that enables different AI systems to integrate with a wide range of services and applications.

Before MCP, developers had to write custom for every new tool or data source they wanted to connect to an AI model. This was not only time-consuming but also led to fragmented systems that were hard to maintain and scale. MCP solves this problem by standardizing these integrations, ensuring that once an AI agent is built with MCP, it can easily communicate with any external system that adheres to the same standard. This standardization unlocks the potential for seamless, secure, and efficient data and tool integration across diverse environments.

How This Book Will Help You Integrate Intelligent Systems

This book is structured to take you from the basics to advanced applications in a step-by-step, tutorial-driven manner. We begin by laying a solid foundation—introducing the fundamental concepts of agentic AI and explaining the rationale behind MCP. As you progress through the chapters, you'll gain a deep understanding of how these technologies work together to empower AI systems.

Here's how the journey will unfold:

- **Clear Explanations:** We'll break down complex ideas into easy-to-understand concepts, using relatable analogies and real-world examples. Picture your AI system as a well-coordinated team where MCP acts as the common language everyone speaks, ensuring smooth collaboration.
- **Logical Progression:** Each chapter builds on the previous one. We start with foundational theories and gradually move into detailed explorations of MCP's architecture, the ecosystem of available tools, and the practical steps required to integrate these systems into your applications.
- **Practical Insights:** Throughout the book, you'll find personal insights and anecdotes that highlight the challenges and breakthroughs in the field of AI integration. These stories are designed to inspire you and provide a realistic picture of what it takes to implement agentic AI in today's technology landscape.
- **Tutorial-Driven Approach:** While we keep technical details accessible, our focus is on guiding you through the conceptual framework first. This way, you'll develop a thorough understanding of the "why" and "how" behind every step before diving into more technical,-based implementations later in your journey.
- **Comprehensive Coverage:** We ensure that no stone is left unturned. From the basics of agentic AI to the intricate details of MCP server architecture, security, real-world applications, and future trends, this book covers every important aspect to give you a complete picture.

By the end of this book, you will not only understand the potential of agentic AI and the transformative power of MCP but also be equipped with the knowledge to apply these technologies in practical, impactful ways. Whether you're looking to innovate in your own projects or simply expand your understanding of the cutting edge of AI, this guide is your roadmap to a future where intelligent systems seamlessly integrate with the world around us.

Welcome to a future where AI agents are not just tools but intelligent collaborators capable of transforming industries, enhancing productivity, and driving innovation. Let's dive in and explore how you can harness this exciting technology to build systems that are not only smart but also truly connected.

Chapter 1: Foundations of Agentic AI and MCP

Welcome to the first chapter of our journey into intelligent systems! In this chapter, we'll lay the groundwork by exploring the basic building blocks: AI agents, the rise of agentic systems, and the Model Context Protocol (MCP). We'll also touch on how to set up these systems without diving into the just yet. Think of this chapter as the blueprint for a futuristic city—understanding the fundamental components that will later be brought to life with detailed instructions.

1.1 What Are AI Agents?

AI agents are, at their core, intelligent software programs designed to perform tasks autonomously, adapt to new information, and interact with their environment much like a human assistant might. They are not merely static algorithms; instead, they learn, evolve, and respond to changing contexts to solve problems, make decisions, and execute actions with minimal human intervention.

Understanding the Core Concept

Imagine having a personal assistant who not only manages your calendar and answers your questions but also anticipates your needs, adapts to your preferences over time, and can take initiative to solve problems before you even notice them. That's the promise of AI agents. They blend the power of data-driven decision-making with the flexibility of adaptive learning to function in dynamic environments—be it in a business setting, a virtual gaming world, or even everyday consumer applications.

Historically, early AI systems were designed around rigid, rule-based frameworks. These systems followed predefined instructions and could only handle very specific tasks. Over time, as machine learning and neural networks advanced, AI systems became more adept at processing complex data, recognizing patterns, and even learning from their own mistakes. This evolution has paved the way for modern AI agents, which leverage vast amounts of data and sophisticated algorithms to continuously improve their performance and adapt to new challenges.

The Evolution of AI Agents

The journey from simple, task-specific programs to today's multifaceted AI agents is marked by several key milestones. In the early days, AI programs could be compared to a set of scripted responses—if you did X, the system would respond with Y. As computational power increased and machine learning techniques matured, these systems gained the ability to process natural language, recognize images, and even mimic certain aspects of human reasoning.

One significant leap in this evolution was the development of reinforcement learning, where AI agents learn optimal behaviors through trial and error in simulated environments. This approach has been instrumental in areas such as robotics and game playing, where agents are required to navigate unpredictable terrains or devise complex strategies. Over time, the integration of these learning methods with more sophisticated models has led to AI agents that can not only execute predefined tasks but also generate new approaches and solutions based on the context they find themselves in.

Types of AI Agents

AI agents can be categorized based on their scope and functionality:

- **Task-Specific Agents:** These are designed to perform a single, narrowly defined function. For example, an AI-powered chatbot that handles customer support inquiries or a scheduling assistant that manages your appointments. Their strength lies in their ability to perform specific tasks with high accuracy, but they may not adapt well outside their designated area.
- **General-Purpose Agents:** Unlike their task-specific counterparts, general-purpose AI agents are built to handle a variety of tasks. They operate much like a Swiss Army knife—versatile and adaptable. These agents can learn from different contexts, switch between tasks, and even integrate multiple functions simultaneously. This adaptability is what makes them particularly exciting in fields where versatility and rapid learning are essential.
- **Collaborative Agents:** In many real-world scenarios, tasks are not performed in isolation. Collaborative agents are designed to work together—either with other AI agents or with human users—to accomplish complex objectives. They communicate, share insights, and adjust their strategies based on collective input. Consider how a team of specialists might work together on a project, each

contributing their expertise to achieve a common goal. Collaborative agents emulate this dynamic, often resulting in outcomes that exceed the sum of their individual capabilities.

Applications of AI Agents

The applications of AI agents are vast and ever-expanding. In customer service, they provide instant responses and handle routine queries, freeing up human employees for more complex tasks. In finance, AI agents are used to analyze market trends, manage portfolios, and even execute trades based on real-time data. In the gaming industry, agents not only enhance gameplay but also create dynamic environments where non-player characters interact in realistic and unexpected ways.

Beyond these examples, AI agents are becoming integral to smart homes, healthcare diagnostics, supply chain management, and even creative fields like art and music production. Their ability to process and analyze large datasets in real time makes them invaluable in environments where rapid, informed decision-making is crucial.

Personal Reflections and Analogies

From my own experience, working with AI agents feels a bit like coaching a sports team. At first, each player (or agent) might only know their position and play by a rigid set of rules. Over time, as they learn from each other and adapt to different game scenarios, they start to coordinate in ways that are truly impressive—anticipating moves, covering for one another, and even innovating new strategies on the fly. This is the beauty of agentic AI: what starts as a simple program can evolve into a dynamic, collaborative system that achieves far more than any single component could on its own.

In summary, AI agents represent a significant leap forward in our quest to create truly intelligent systems. They are the building blocks of modern automation, capable of learning, adapting, and collaborating to solve problems in real time. As we explore further into this book, we'll see how these agents can be integrated with external tools through the Model Context Protocol, unlocking even greater potential for innovation and efficiency.

By understanding the evolution, types, and practical applications of AI agents, you're taking the first step toward mastering a technology that is reshaping our world. Let's continue our exploration, building on this foundation to delve deeper into the interconnected ecosystem of agentic AI and MCP.

1.2 The Rise of Agentic Systems

Agentic systems have come a long way from their humble beginnings, evolving into sophisticated, dynamic entities that are reshaping how we approach automation, decision-making, and collaboration in various industries. This section delves into the historical evolution of these systems, highlights the key milestones that paved the way for today's intelligent agents, and examines their transformative impact on diverse sectors.

Historical Context and Evolution

The journey of agentic systems began with early computing efforts where machines performed strictly defined tasks based on pre-written rules. In those days, if you wanted a computer to solve a problem, you had to lay out every single step in painstaking detail—much like following a recipe without any room for improvisation. These early systems were powerful for specific tasks but were inherently rigid and unable to adapt to new challenges.

As computational power increased and the fields of machine learning and artificial intelligence began to mature, researchers started exploring ways to create systems that could learn from data and adapt over time. A major breakthrough came with the development of neural networks, which allowed machines to recognize patterns in data without being explicitly programmed for every eventuality. This laid the groundwork for systems that could begin to mimic human learning, gradually shifting from static rule-based processes to more fluid, adaptable behaviors.

The introduction of reinforcement learning further propelled this evolution. In reinforcement learning, agents learn by interacting with an environment and receiving feedback in the form of rewards or penalties. It's much like training a pet—through consistent feedback, the agent gradually understands which actions yield positive outcomes. Over time, these agents learn to optimize their behavior, often discovering creative strategies to achieve their goals. This learning paradigm was particularly transformative in simulated environments, such as video games and robotics, where agents could experiment and refine their actions in real time.

Milestones in the Rise of Agentic Systems

Several key milestones have marked the rise of agentic systems:

- **Early Rule-Based Systems:** Initially, systems were limited to executing predefined instructions. While groundbreaking at the time, these systems could not handle unexpected inputs or adapt to changing conditions.
- **Advent of Machine Learning:** The shift towards machine learning allowed systems to learn from experience. Early neural networks demonstrated that machines could start to recognize patterns in data, setting the stage for more advanced learning.
- **Reinforcement Learning Breakthroughs:** Reinforcement learning introduced a dynamic method for training agents through trial and error, enabling them to develop strategies in complex environments such as simulated games and robotic navigation.
- **Integration of Natural Language Processing:** With advancements in NLP, agents began to understand and generate human-like language. This made them more interactive and capable of engaging in meaningful conversations, a leap forward in making AI agents more accessible and useful.
- **Emergence of Collaborative Systems:** Today's agentic systems are not isolated; they are designed to work in concert with one another and with human users. This collaborative aspect is critical, as it enables the creation of systems where agents can share insights, coordinate tasks, and even compensate for each other's limitations.

Transformative Impact on Industries

The evolution of agentic systems has had a profound impact across multiple industries, transforming workflows and redefining traditional roles. In finance, for instance, AI agents now monitor markets and execute trades at speeds and accuracies far beyond human capabilities. These agents analyze vast amounts of real-time data to make split-second decisions, often leading to more efficient and effective investment strategies.

In healthcare, agentic systems are being used to support diagnostic processes, manage patient data, and even assist in personalized treatment plans. The ability of these agents to sift through complex medical records and extract meaningful insights can lead to earlier diagnoses and better outcomes for patients.

Manufacturing and logistics have also seen significant benefits. Here, AI agents coordinate production lines, manage inventory, and optimize supply chains. They work alongside human workers, streamlining operations and reducing errors. In customer service, intelligent agents handle routine inquiries and support tasks, freeing up human employees to tackle more nuanced problems and drive strategic initiatives.

One striking example comes from the world of gaming. Consider virtual environments where AI agents not only simulate human behavior but also create dynamic, emergent gameplay. In projects like the Sid simulation, thousands of AI agents interact within a virtual world—building economies, forming communities, and even establishing governance systems. Such experiments reveal the potential of agentic systems to mimic complex human social structures and decision-making processes, offering insights that could eventually be applied in more critical real-world scenarios.

Personal Insights and Reflections

Working with agentic systems can often feel like witnessing the evolution of a living ecosystem. I recall the first time I observed an AI agent learning to navigate a complex virtual maze—it was as if the system was discovering its own path, much like a child exploring a new playground. There was a moment of awe when the agent, through trial and error, developed an unconventional yet efficient route to the goal, demonstrating creativity that wasn't explicitly programmed.

Such experiences underscore the transformative potential of these systems. They're not just about automating tasks; they're about creating systems that learn, adapt, and evolve in ways that can eventually mirror human ingenuity. This evolution isn't merely technological—it's a shift in how we conceptualize intelligence and problem-solving in the digital age.

Looking Ahead

As we continue to see rapid advancements in AI, the role of agentic systems is only set to grow. Their ability to autonomously integrate new data, learn from complex environments, and collaborate with other agents and humans positions them as key drivers of innovation across virtually every industry. The transformative impact of these systems is already evident, and as they become more refined, we can expect them to tackle even more challenging tasks, opening up new possibilities for efficiency, creativity, and human-AI collaboration.

In the next sections of this book, we will build on these foundational insights, exploring how the Model Context Protocol (MCP) further amplifies the capabilities of agentic systems by providing a standardized way to integrate diverse tools and data sources. The future of intelligent systems is interconnected, adaptive, and dynamic—and agentic systems lie at the heart of this exciting evolution.

1.3 Introducing the Model Context Protocol (MCP)

Imagine trying to connect a variety of devices—each with its own unique plug and interface—to your computer. In the past, this was a challenge that required a maze of adapters and cables. Today, the universal USB-C standard has simplified these connections, ensuring that almost every modern device can communicate with your computer using one common interface. The Model Context Protocol (MCP) serves a similar purpose for AI agents, providing a standardized, universal framework that connects these systems to the myriad of external data sources and tools they need to perform at their best.

The Need for Standardization

In the early days of AI, developers had to write custom integrations for every new data source or tool an AI model needed to access. This approach was like building a unique bridge for every river you encountered—effective for a single use case but unsustainable at scale. Each custom integration required significant time, effort, and maintenance. As AI models grew in complexity and capability, the limitations of this ad hoc approach became glaringly obvious. The fragmented landscape hindered not only rapid development but also the scalability and security of AI systems.

MCP emerged as a solution to these challenges. Its primary goal is to establish a common "language" or protocol through which AI agents can interact seamlessly with various external systems. By doing so, MCP eliminates the need for repetitive, one-off integrations and opens the door to a more streamlined, efficient, and secure method of connecting intelligent systems with the data and tools they rely on.

The Architecture of MCP

At its core, MCP is built on a simple yet powerful client–server architecture that mirrors the logic of many successful communication protocols. Here's how it breaks down:

- **MCP Hosts:** These are the AI agents or applications that require access to external resources. Think of them as the users in our universal adapter analogy—each needing to plug into the network to perform their tasks.
- **MCP Clients:** Acting as intermediaries, these clients manage the communication between the AI agents and the external tools or data sources. They ensure that requests and responses follow a standardized format, which is crucial for interoperability.
- **MCP Servers:** These servers expose specific functionalities or data from external systems. Whether it's accessing a database, retrieving information from a web API, or interfacing with local file systems, MCP servers act as the gateway that provides these capabilities in a consistent, secure manner.

This architecture ensures that once an AI agent is integrated with MCP, it can tap into a wide range of services without needing a new integration for each one. The protocol uses standardized communication—often leveraging formats like JSON-RPC—to handle requests and responses, which helps maintain clarity and security across interactions.

Benefits Over Traditional Integration Methods

One of the biggest advantages of MCP is its ability to reduce complexity. Traditionally, integrating an AI system with external tools involved bespoke coding for every new service—a process prone to errors and difficult to maintain. MCP, by contrast, provides a "plug-and-play" solution. Once an external service adheres to the MCP standard, any MCP-compatible AI agent can use it immediately.

Here are some of the tangible benefits:

- **Interoperability:** With MCP, the same standard is used across diverse systems. This uniformity allows AI agents to easily switch between different providers or services without the need for rewriting integration.
- **Scalability:** Standardized protocols simplify the process of adding new tools and data sources. This means that as your needs grow, your

system can scale seamlessly, much like adding more USB-C devices to your modern laptop.

- **Security:** By consolidating integrations into a standardized framework, MCP makes it easier to implement and enforce robust security measures. Instead of patching individual integrations, developers can focus on securing a unified protocol.
- **Efficiency:** MCP reduces redundancy. Instead of duplicating similar for each new integration, developers can reuse existing MCP-compliant tools, accelerating development cycles and reducing maintenance overhead.

A Real-World Analogy

To further clarify, imagine building a smart home. In a traditional setup, each device—be it a thermostat, a light bulb, or a security camera—might come with its own app and require separate wiring or connections. Managing such a diverse array of systems can be overwhelming. However, with a smart home hub that uses a common protocol, all your devices can be controlled from a single interface, communicating smoothly with one another. MCP is that hub for AI agents. It ensures that all external systems—no matter how different—can connect and work together seamlessly, creating a cohesive ecosystem where each component enhances the performance of the whole.

Personal Reflections on MCP's Potential

In my experience, working with systems that leverage standardized protocols has always felt like turning chaos into order. Early in my career, I encountered multiple instances where disparate systems failed to communicate efficiently, resulting in repeated headaches and frustrating delays. Adopting a standardized method not only streamlined these processes but also opened up new possibilities for innovation. MCP promises to bring that same level of transformation to AI integration.

For those of us who have witnessed the evolution of technology—from the cumbersome, fragmented systems of the past to the unified, efficient solutions of today—MCP represents a logical and exciting next step. It's a tool that doesn't just improve the way AI agents work; it fundamentally changes the landscape, making it easier for these agents to access and leverage the full spectrum of digital resources available.

Looking Forward

As we move further into this book, we will explore how to implement and utilize MCP in practical scenarios. Whether you're aiming to build advanced trading agents, develop dynamic virtual environments, or streamline enterprise workflows, MCP provides a solid foundation upon which you can build robust, intelligent systems. The protocol is not just a technical standard—it's a catalyst for innovation, opening up a world where AI agents can truly connect, collaborate, and elevate their functionality.

In the upcoming chapters, we'll dive deeper into the specifics of MCP's architecture, explore various MCP servers and frameworks, and guide you through the practical steps needed to harness this powerful protocol. With MCP, the future of AI integration is not only within reach—it's here, ready to revolutionize the way we build and interact with intelligent systems.

1.4 Installation and Setups

Setting up your MCP environment correctly is critical for integrating intelligent AI agents with external data sources and tools. In this section, we walk through every step needed to install and configure both Python-based and Node.js-based MCP servers. By following these instructions, you'll create a robust development environment that supports seamless integration and scalable deployment.

Step 1: System Requirements and Prerequisites

Before proceeding with the installation, ensure that your system meets the following requirements:

- **Python 3.9+** installed (for Python-based MCP servers).
- **Node.js and npm** installed (for Node.js-based MCP servers).
- **Git** for cloning repositories.
- A stable internet connection to download dependencies.

For Windows, macOS, or Linux, visit the official websites of Python and Node.js to download and install the latest versions. If you prefer a package manager, use Homebrew on macOS or your Linux distribution's package manager.

Step 2: Installing Required Software

For Python-based MCP Servers:

1. **Install Python:**
   Verify your installation by running:

```bash
python --version
```

   Ensure that it prints a version number 3.9 or higher.

2. **Install uvx:**
   MCP servers written in Python often use uvx for a streamlined development experience. Install it using pip:

```bash
pip install uvx
```

   This tool simplifies running MCP server commands via the command line.

3. **Clone an MCP Server Repository:**
   Many MCP servers are available on GitHub. For instance, to work with a filesystem integration server, clone the repository:

```bash
git clone
https://github.com/modelcontextprotocol/servers.git
cd servers
```

   Navigate to the directory of the Python-based MCP server you want to use (e.g., mcp-server-filesystem).

4. **Install the MCP Server Package:**
   Assuming the repository provides a Python package, install it using pip:

```bash
```

```
pip install -e .
```

The -e flag installs the package in editable mode, allowing you to make changes and test them without reinstalling.

For Node.js-based MCP Servers:

1. **Install Node.js and npm:**
   Confirm installation with:

```bash

node --version
npm --version
```

   Both commands should return version numbers indicating successful installation.

2. **Using npx for Quick Setup:**
   Many Node.js-based MCP servers can be executed directly with npx, which comes with npm. For example, if you are using an MCP server for web content fetching, run:

```bash

npx -y @modelcontextprotocol/server-fetch
```

   This command automatically downloads and executes the package without a full installation.

Step 3: Running an MCP Server

Below are detailed examples for running both a Python-based and a Node.js-based MCP server.

Python Example: Running a Filesystem MCP Server

1. **Open your terminal and navigate to the MCP server directory:**

```bash

```

```
cd path/to/mcp-server-filesystem
```

2. **Run the MCP Server using uvx:**

```bash
uvx mcp-server-filesystem
```

As the server starts, you will see output indicating that it is listening on a specific port (commonly via STDIO). This confirms that the MCP server is up and running.

3. **Verify the Server:**
Use your browser or a terminal-based tool like `curl` to check if the server is responding. For example:

```bash
curl http://localhost:8000/status
```

A JSON response should confirm that the server is active.

Node.js Example: Running a Fetch MCP Server

1. **Run the Server Directly with npx:**

```bash
npx -y @modelcontextprotocol/server-fetch
```

The command fetches the package, runs it, and displays logs in the terminal. You should see a message indicating the server is ready for connections.

2. **Check the Output:**
Look for specific log entries that denote successful initialization. The server might list available tools or provide status messages confirming that it is operational.

Step 4: Configuring MCP Client Settings

After setting up your MCP server, the next step is to connect it to your MCP client (e.g., an AI agent interface such as Claude Desktop). Although detailed client integration comes in later chapters, it is useful to understand the basic configuration process.

1. **Create a Configuration File:**
   Typically, you'll need to define a JSON configuration that maps your MCP server command and arguments. For example:

```json
{
  "mcpServers": {
    "filesystem": {
      "command": "uvx",
      "args": ["mcp-server-filesystem", "--port",
"8000"]
    },
    "fetch": {
      "command": "npx",
      "args": ["-y", "@modelcontextprotocol/server-
fetch"]
    }
  }
}
```

   Save this configuration file in the directory where your MCP client expects it, often within a designated configuration folder.

2. **Environment Variables:**
   In some cases, the MCP server might require environment variables for authentication or to specify resource paths. You can set these variables in your shell or within a .env file. For example:

```bash
export MCP_API_KEY=your_api_key_here
export FILESYSTEM_PATH=/absolute/path/to/allowed/files
```

   Loading these variables ensures that the MCP server has the necessary context to operate securely.

3. **Testing the Connection:**
   Use a simple client command (or the built-in test feature of your MCP client) to confirm that the server responds appropriately. This

might involve invoking a "list tools" endpoint via the MCP client interface, which should return a structured list of available functions.

Step 5: Practical Tips and Troubleshooting

- **Documentation and Logs:**
  Always refer to the official documentation of the MCP server you are using. Log output is invaluable for identifying issues. If the server isn't starting as expected, check for error messages that can guide you to missing dependencies or configuration errors.
- **Consistency Across Environments:**
  Whether you're developing on your local machine or deploying to a cloud service, ensure that your environment configurations remain consistent. Containerization with Docker can help standardize your setup across different platforms.
- **Testing Incrementally:**
  Start by running a basic version of your MCP server, and gradually add more features. This incremental approach makes it easier to pinpoint problems and ensures that each component works as intended before integrating them into a larger system.
- **Community and Support:**
  Engage with the community through forums or GitHub repositories related to MCP. Many issues you encounter might have already been addressed by other developers, and community-driven documentation can offer practical insights.

Conclusion

Setting up an MCP server is a foundational step in integrating intelligent AI systems with the external tools and data they need to operate effectively. This guide provided a comprehensive, step-by-step walkthrough—from system prerequisites and software installation to running the server and configuring client settings. With these steps in place, you'll have a robust development environment that lays the groundwork for building advanced, agentic AI solutions. As you move forward in this book, the environment you've set up here will serve as the launchpad for more complex integrations and practical applications of MCP.

Chapter 2: MCP Architecture and Communication Protocols

In this chapter, we explore the inner workings of the Model Context Protocol (MCP), a foundational component that enables intelligent systems to interact with external tools and data in a standardized, secure, and efficient manner. By understanding the architecture of MCP and the communication protocols it leverages, you'll gain valuable insights into how to build robust, scalable, and interoperable AI integrations. This chapter is structured into three key sections: an overview of the MCP architecture, an exploration of its communication mechanisms, and a discussion on the standardization and interoperability that make MCP a powerful tool in modern AI systems.

2.1 Overview of MCP Architecture

The Model Context Protocol (MCP) is built on a simple yet powerful client–server model that enables seamless communication between AI agents and external services. In this section, we will explore the three primary components of MCP—Hosts, Clients, and Servers—and detail their roles within the ecosystem. We'll illustrate these concepts using practical, step-by-step examples that demonstrate how each component interacts in a real-world scenario.

MCP Hosts, Clients, and Servers: Key Components and Their Roles

- **MCP Hosts:**
  These are the AI agents or applications that initiate requests. They represent the "front end" of your intelligent system. An MCP host might be a chatbot, a trading agent, or any other application that needs to access external tools or data.
- **MCP Clients:**
  Acting as intermediaries, MCP clients manage the connection between the host and the server. They format requests according to the MCP standard (often using JSON-RPC) and ensure that responses are delivered back in a compatible format.
- **MCP Servers:**
  These are the services that expose external functionalities or data

20

sources. An MCP server could interface with a file system, a database, an API, or any other resource. It processes the requests from the client and returns the necessary data or performs the required action.

To understand how these components work together, consider an analogy with a restaurant:

- The **host** is the customer placing an order.
- The **client** is the waiter who takes the order and communicates it to the kitchen.
- The **server** is the kitchen where the food is prepared and then delivered back through the waiter to the customer.

This architecture not only simplifies integration but also standardizes the communication process, making it easier to scale and maintain your AI systems.

Practical Implementation

Below are three functional examples written in Python that illustrate how an MCP Host, Client, and Server can be set up and interact using JSON-RPC.

Example 1: Building an MCP Server

In this example, we use Flask to create a simple MCP server that exposes a single method, `get_status()`, which returns the server's current status.

```python
# mcp_server.py

from flask import Flask, request, jsonify
import json
from datetime import datetime

app = Flask(__name__)

@app.route('/jsonrpc', methods=['POST'])
def jsonrpc():
    try:
        # Parse the incoming JSON-RPC request
```

```
        req = request.get_json()
        method = req.get('method')
        params = req.get('params', {})
        id_ = req.get('id')

        # Process the request based on the method
        if method == 'get_status':
            result = {
                "status": "running",
                "timestamp": datetime.utcnow().isoformat() +
"Z"
            }
        else:
            return jsonify({
                "jsonrpc": "2.0",
                "error": {"code": -32601, "message": "Method
not found"},
                "id": id_
            })

        # Return the JSON-RPC response
        return jsonify({
            "jsonrpc": "2.0",
            "result": result,
            "id": id_
        })
    except Exception as e:
        return jsonify({
            "jsonrpc": "2.0",
            "error": {"code": -32603, "message": str(e)},
            "id": None
        })

if __name__ == '__main__':
    # Run the server on localhost port 5000
    app.run(host='127.0.0.1', port=5000)
```

Explanation:

- The Flask app listens for POST requests on the /jsonrpc endpoint.
- When a request is received, it checks the method field. If the method is get_status, it returns the server status and the current UTC timestamp.
- If an unknown method is requested, the server responds with a JSON-RPC error message.

Example 2: Creating an MCP Client

Next, we implement an MCP client that sends a JSON-RPC request to the server. The client uses the `requests` library to perform an HTTP POST.

```python
python

# mcp_client.py

import requests
import json

def call_mcp_method(url, method, params=None, request_id=1):
    # Build the JSON-RPC request payload
    payload = {
        "jsonrpc": "2.0",
        "method": method,
        "params": params if params is not None else {},
        "id": request_id
    }
    headers = {'Content-Type': 'application/json'}

    # Send the request to the MCP server
    response = requests.post(url, data=json.dumps(payload),
headers=headers)

    # Parse and return the JSON response
    return response.json()

# Example usage
if __name__ == "__main__":
    server_url = "http://127.0.0.1:5000/jsonrpc"
    response = call_mcp_method(server_url, "get_status")
    print("MCP Server Response:", response)
```

Explanation:

- The `call_mcp_method` function constructs a JSON-RPC compliant request with a specified method and parameters.
- The function sends this payload to the MCP server URL and returns the parsed JSON response.
- Running this script while the MCP server is active will print out the server's status and timestamp.

Example 3: Implementing an MCP Host

Finally, the MCP host integrates the client functionality. In a real-world scenario, the host could be an AI agent that needs to retrieve the server status as part of its operations.

```python
python

# mcp_host.py

from mcp_client import call_mcp_method

def main():
    # Define the MCP server endpoint
    server_url = "http://127.0.0.1:5000/jsonrpc"

    # The host (e.g., an AI agent) makes a request to get the
server status
    print("Requesting server status from MCP Server...")
    response = call_mcp_method(server_url, "get_status")

    # Process and display the response
    if "result" in response:
        status = response["result"]
        print("Server is:", status["status"])
        print("Current Timestamp (UTC):",
status["timestamp"])
    else:
        print("Error:", response.get("error", "Unknown
error"))

if __name__ == "__main__":
    main()
```

Explanation:

- The MCP host script imports the client function and uses it to send a request to the MCP server.
- It processes the returned JSON response, displaying the server's status and current timestamp.
- This simple example demonstrates how an AI agent (the host) can leverage the MCP client to access functionalities provided by an MCP server.

Commentary and Key Insights

The above examples illustrate the core concepts of MCP architecture in a practical, step-by-step manner. By separating the system into three distinct components—host, client, and server—we ensure that each part of the process is modular and maintainable. The use of JSON-RPC for communication standardizes the data exchange, making it easier to integrate multiple servers and tools without having to reinvent the wheel each time.

From my own experience, implementing standardized protocols like MCP significantly reduces integration overhead. I've seen teams struggle with custom connectors for every new data source, and once a standard is in place, development becomes much more efficient and less error-prone. The simplicity of the examples above reflects the power of such standardization: a few clear, well-documented lines can replace hours of custom development work.

Conclusion

This section has provided a comprehensive overview of the MCP architecture, detailing the roles of hosts, clients, and servers, and how they work together using standardized communication protocols. The practical examples demonstrate a complete, functional implementation from server setup to client communication and host integration. With this foundation, you are well-prepared to explore more advanced aspects of MCP integration in later chapters.

2.2 Communication Mechanisms

The Model Context Protocol (MCP) uses specific communication mechanisms to enable seamless interactions between AI agents and external tools. Two primary methods are employed: STDIO transport for local integrations and Server-Sent Events (SSE) for remote interactions. In this section, we explain each mechanism in detail and provide complete, functional examples to illustrate how they work in practice.

STDIO Transport for Local Integrations

STDIO (Standard Input/Output) is a straightforward mechanism often used when your MCP server and client run on the same machine. This method leverages the system's input and output streams to exchange messages.

Because there is no network overhead, STDIO is highly efficient for local development, testing, and scenarios where rapid communication is required.

How STDIO Transport Works

With STDIO, the MCP server reads incoming requests from standard input (stdin) and sends responses to standard output (stdout). The client, in turn, spawns the server process, writes the request data to its stdin, and captures the server's stdout to process the response. This direct communication is analogous to having a conversation face-to-face, with minimal delay.

Example: Building a Simple STDIO-Based MCP Server and Client

Below are two Python scripts that demonstrate a basic implementation using STDIO.

Server Script (stdio_server.py):

```python
#!/usr/bin/env python3
"""
A simple MCP server that uses STDIO to read JSON-RPC requests
from stdin
and writes JSON-RPC responses to stdout.
"""

import sys
import json
from datetime import datetime

def process_request(request):
    """
    Process the JSON-RPC request and return a response.

    Parameters:
        request (dict): The JSON-RPC request object.

    Returns:
        dict: The JSON-RPC response object.
    """
    method = request.get("method")
    request_id = request.get("id")

    # Example: support only the 'get_status' method.
    if method == "get_status":
        result = {
```

```python
                "status": "running",
                "timestamp": datetime.utcnow().isoformat() + "Z"
            }
        response = {
            "jsonrpc": "2.0",
            "result": result,
            "id": request_id
        }
    else:
        response = {
            "jsonrpc": "2.0",
            "error": {"code": -32601, "message": "Method not
found"},
            "id": request_id
        }
    return response

def main():
    # Read a line from stdin
    raw_request = sys.stdin.readline()
    if not raw_request:
        return

    try:
        request = json.loads(raw_request)
    except json.JSONDecodeError as e:
        error_response = {
            "jsonrpc": "2.0",
            "error": {"code": -32700, "message": "Parse
error: " + str(e)},
            "id": None
        }
        sys.stdout.write(json.dumps(error_response) + "\n")
        sys.stdout.flush()
        return

    # Process the request and write the response to stdout
    response = process_request(request)
    sys.stdout.write(json.dumps(response) + "\n")
    sys.stdout.flush()

if __name__ == "__main__":
    main()
```

Explanation:

- This server script reads a single JSON-RPC request from `stdin`,
  processes it by checking if the method is `"get_status"`, and

responds with a JSON object containing the server's status and current UTC timestamp.
- The response is written to stdout and flushed to ensure the client receives it immediately.

Client Script (stdio_client.py):

```python
python

#!/usr/bin/env python3
"""
A simple MCP client that spawns the STDIO-based MCP server,
sends a JSON-RPC request, and prints the response.
"""

import subprocess
import json

def call_stdio_server(server_script, method, params=None,
request_id=1):
    """
    Call the MCP server using STDIO transport.

    Parameters:
        server_script (str): Path to the MCP server script.
        method (str): The JSON-RPC method to invoke.
        params (dict, optional): Parameters for the method.
        request_id (int): Unique request identifier.

    Returns:
        dict: The server's JSON-RPC response.
    """
    # Build the JSON-RPC request payload
    payload = {
        "jsonrpc": "2.0",
        "method": method,
        "params": params if params is not None else {},
        "id": request_id
    }
    # Start the server process
    process = subprocess.Popen(
        ["python3", server_script],
        stdin=subprocess.PIPE,
        stdout=subprocess.PIPE,
        text=True
    )
    # Send the request payload to the server's stdin
    stdout_data, _ = process.communicate(json.dumps(payload)
+ "\n")
```

```
    # Parse the server's response
    return json.loads(stdout_data)

if __name__ == "__main__":
    server_path = "stdio_server.py"
    response = call_stdio_server(server_path, "get_status")
    print("Server Response:", response)
```

Explanation:

- The client script builds a JSON-RPC request to call the `get_status` method.
- It spawns the MCP server as a subprocess, sends the JSON payload via `stdin`, and then reads the response from `stdout`.
- Finally, the JSON response is parsed and printed. This demonstrates a clear, direct way to communicate with an MCP server using STDIO.

SSE Transport for Remote Interactions

Server-Sent Events (SSE) is designed for scenarios where your MCP server is hosted remotely, such as on a cloud server. SSE allows the server to push updates to the client over an HTTP connection, which is particularly useful for real-time data feeds or long-running processes.

How SSE Transport Works

With SSE, the server maintains an HTTP connection and continuously sends data (events) to the client as new information becomes available. This is similar to receiving live updates on a news ticker, where the client doesn't have to repeatedly request new data; instead, the server streams it in real time. This approach is ideal for applications requiring timely updates, such as live monitoring systems or interactive web applications.

Example: Implementing an SSE Server and Client

Below are examples of an SSE server built with Flask and a corresponding Python client that listens for events.

SSE Server Script (sse_server.py):

```python
#!/usr/bin/env python3
"""
A simple SSE server using Flask that streams server status
updates.
"""

from flask import Flask, Response
import time
import json
from datetime import datetime

app = Flask(__name__)

def event_stream():
    """
    Generator function that yields server status updates as
SSE events.
    """
    while True:
        # Construct the event data with current status and
timestamp
        data = {
            "status": "running",
            "timestamp": datetime.utcnow().isoformat() + "Z"
        }
        # Format the SSE event
        event = f"data: {json.dumps(data)}\n\n"
        yield event
        time.sleep(5)   # Send an update every 5 seconds

@app.route('/sse')
def sse():
    """
    SSE endpoint that streams status updates.
    """
    return Response(event_stream(), mimetype='text/event-
stream')

if __name__ == "__main__":
    app.run(host='0.0.0.0', port=5001)
```

Explanation:

- The Flask-based SSE server defines an endpoint /sse that streams JSON-formatted server status updates every 5 seconds.

- The `event_stream` generator function creates an infinite loop that yields formatted SSE events, which are then sent to any connected client.

SSE Client Script (sse_client.py):

```python
#!/usr/bin/env python3
"""
A simple SSE client that connects to the SSE server and
prints incoming events.
"""

import requests
import sseclient
import json

def listen_to_sse(url):
    """
    Connects to the SSE server at the given URL and listens
    for events.

    Parameters:
        url (str): The URL of the SSE endpoint.
    """
    # Establish a streaming HTTP request to the SSE endpoint
    response = requests.get(url, stream=True)
    # Use sseclient to parse the event stream
    client = sseclient.SSEClient(response)

    for event in client.events():
        try:
            data = json.loads(event.data)
            print("Received Event:", data)
        except json.JSONDecodeError:
            print("Received non-JSON event:", event.data)

if __name__ == "__main__":
    sse_url = "http://127.0.0.1:5001/sse"
    print("Connecting to SSE server...")
    listen_to_sse(sse_url)
```

Explanation:

- The SSE client script connects to the SSE endpoint using the `requests` library with streaming enabled.

31

- The `sseclient` library is then used to parse the incoming event stream.
- For each event received, the script attempts to decode the JSON data and prints it to the console. This setup demonstrates how an MCP client can receive continuous, real-time updates from a remote server.

Commentary and Key Insights

Implementing communication mechanisms through STDIO and SSE in MCP environments showcases how different scenarios call for distinct approaches. STDIO is perfect for local, direct interactions where simplicity and speed are essential, while SSE is tailored for remote environments, enabling continuous, real-time data streaming over HTTP.

These two methods not only illustrate the versatility of MCP but also emphasize the importance of choosing the right communication strategy based on your deployment context. My personal experiences in setting up similar systems have underscored the benefits of these approaches—STDIO for its straightforwardness during early development and testing, and SSE for its robust performance in production environments where live updates are crucial.

Conclusion

This section provided a detailed exploration of the communication mechanisms used in MCP, with complete, functional examples for both STDIO and SSE transports. By following the step-by-step examples, you now have a clear understanding of how to implement local and remote communication channels within your MCP ecosystem. These mechanisms are fundamental to creating scalable and efficient AI integrations, paving the way for more advanced applications in subsequent chapters.

2.3 Standardization and Interoperability

Standardization and interoperability are cornerstones of the Model Context Protocol (MCP), ensuring that disparate systems can communicate seamlessly. By adopting a common protocol—most notably JSON-RPC along with well-defined schema definitions—MCP enables AI agents and external services to exchange data reliably and securely. This chapter explains the principles behind standardization, details the role of JSON-RPC and schema definitions, and demonstrates how a unified protocol simplifies integration through practical, step-by-step examples.

The Role of Standardization in MCP

In any complex ecosystem, inconsistent interfaces can lead to fragmented systems that are hard to maintain and scale. With MCP, the idea is to create a "universal language" for AI integrations. Rather than building a custom connector for every tool or data source, developers can leverage the MCP standard. This common framework ensures that any component adhering to the protocol can interact with another, much like different devices communicating via a universal adapter.

Standardization here is achieved primarily through JSON-RPC, a lightweight remote procedure call protocol that uses JSON to encode messages. With JSON-RPC, both requests and responses follow a consistent format, which is further enforced by schema definitions. These schemas act as contracts, outlining exactly what data each message should contain. As a result, the process of validation is streamlined, reducing errors and making it easier for systems to interoperate.

JSON-RPC and Schema Definitions

JSON-RPC provides a structured way to handle function calls across a network. Every message includes a few critical components:

- **jsonrpc:** Specifies the protocol version (typically "2.0").
- **method:** The name of the method to be invoked.
- **params:** The parameters required for the method.
- **id:** A unique identifier for the request, used to match responses.

Schema definitions go hand-in-hand with JSON-RPC by ensuring that the data exchanged conforms to expected formats. This is particularly important in MCP, where multiple systems must reliably interpret the same messages. Validating these messages against a schema prevents miscommunication and ensures that both ends of the connection can process the data correctly.

Benefits of a Unified Protocol

Using a standardized protocol such as MCP offers several practical benefits:

- **Interoperability:** An AI agent built to communicate via MCP can interact with any MCP-compliant server, regardless of its internal implementation. This uniformity drastically reduces integration efforts.
- **Reduced Redundancy:** Developers need to write the integration only once, then reuse it across multiple tools and data sources.
- **Enhanced Security:** A centralized protocol makes it easier to implement consistent security measures, such as authentication and input validation, across all connections.
- **Maintainability and Scalability:** With a unified protocol, updates and changes are propagated across all systems, making it easier to scale and maintain large, interconnected ecosystems.

Practical Implementation: JSON-RPC Request Validation

To illustrate the power of standardization and interoperability, consider a Python example where we define and validate a JSON-RPC request using schema definitions. This example uses the `jsonschema` library to enforce the structure of our JSON-RPC messages.

Step 1: Define the JSON-RPC Request Schema

Create a file named `json_rpc_schema.py` with the following:

```python
import jsonschema
import json

# Define the JSON-RPC 2.0 request schema
json_rpc_request_schema = {
    "type": "object",
    "properties": {
        "jsonrpc": {
            "type": "string",
```

```python
            "pattern": "^2\\.0$"   # Ensures the version is
exactly "2.0"
        },
        "method": {"type": "string"},
        "params": {"type": ["object", "array"], "default":
{}},
        "id": {"anyOf": [{"type": "number"}, {"type":
"string"}, {"type": "null"}]}
    },
    "required": ["jsonrpc", "method", "id"],
    "additionalProperties": False
}

def validate_request(request_data):
    """
    Validate a JSON-RPC request against the defined schema.

    Parameters:
        request_data (dict): The JSON-RPC request to
validate.

    Raises:
        jsonschema.ValidationError: If the request does not
conform to the schema.
    """
    jsonschema.validate(instance=request_data,
schema=json_rpc_request_schema)
    print("Validation succeeded for:", request_data)

if __name__ == "__main__":
    # Example of a valid JSON-RPC request
    valid_request = {
        "jsonrpc": "2.0",
        "method": "get_status",
        "params": {"detail": "full"},
        "id": 1
    }
    validate_request(valid_request)

    # Example of an invalid JSON-RPC request (incorrect JSON-
RPC version)
    invalid_request = {
        "jsonrpc": "1.0",
        "method": "get_status",
        "id": 1
    }
    try:
        validate_request(invalid_request)
    except jsonschema.ValidationError as e:
        print("Validation error:", e.message)
```

Explanation:

- **Schema Definition:** The JSON schema is defined to strictly adhere to JSON-RPC 2.0, ensuring that the `jsonrpc` property matches the pattern `"2.0"`, and requiring the `method` and `id` fields.
- **Validation Function:** The `validate_request` function uses `jsonschema.validate()` to check if a given JSON object conforms to the schema. If it does, a success message is printed; otherwise, a `ValidationError` is raised.
- **Example Usage:** Two examples demonstrate validation—one that passes and one that fails due to an incorrect JSON-RPC version.

Step 2: Using the Schema in an MCP Client

Once the schema is defined, any MCP client can use it to validate outgoing or incoming messages, ensuring that both sides of the communication adhere to the standard. This not only reduces errors but also simplifies debugging and integration when multiple systems interact.

Below is a conceptual snippet that shows how an MCP client might incorporate this validation before sending a request:

```python
import json
from json_rpc_schema import json_rpc_request_schema,
validate_request

def prepare_request(method, params=None, request_id=1):
    """
    Prepare a JSON-RPC request and validate it against the
schema.

    Parameters:
        method (str): The method to call.
        params (dict or list, optional): The parameters for
the method.
        request_id (int, str, or None): A unique identifier
for the request.

    Returns:
        dict: A valid JSON-RPC request.
    """
    request = {
        "jsonrpc": "2.0",
        "method": method,
```

```
        "params": params if params is not None else {},
        "id": request_id
    }
    # Validate the request before sending
    validate_request(request)
    return request

# Example usage:
if __name__ == "__main__":
    request_payload = prepare_request("get_status",
{"detail": "full"}, request_id=42)
    print("Prepared Request:", json.dumps(request_payload,
indent=2))
```

Explanation:

- **Request Preparation:** The `prepare_request` function constructs a JSON-RPC request using the given parameters.
- **Validation Step:** Before returning the request, it calls `validate_request()` to ensure the payload meets the standardized format.
- **Output:** Running this produces a validated, well-structured JSON-RPC request that can be sent over the network.

Commentary and Key Insights

Standardization using JSON-RPC and schema definitions offers clear benefits for interoperability in MCP. By enforcing a uniform message format, MCP ensures that every component—from the AI agent (host) to the external service (server)—speaks the same language. This reduces the chances of miscommunication and simplifies the development process across diverse systems. In my experience, having a rigorous validation layer early in the integration process saves considerable time by catching errors before they propagate through the system.

Conclusion

This section has provided a detailed look at how standardization and interoperability are achieved in MCP through JSON-RPC and schema definitions. The provided examples demonstrate, step by step, how to define a JSON schema, validate requests, and integrate these validations into an MCP client workflow. With these standardized protocols in place, you can be confident that your AI agents will interact smoothly with external tools and data sources, laying a solid foundation for building robust, scalable intelligent systems.

Chapter 3: The MCP Ecosystem and Tooling

The MCP ecosystem is a vibrant and expanding network of tools, servers, and frameworks that empower AI agents to interact seamlessly with external resources. This chapter provides an in-depth look at the various components that form this ecosystem, from official implementations and curated community projects to specialized frameworks that simplify development. We will also examine practical case studies that showcase how MCP-enabled AI agents perform in simulated environments like Minecraft and in real-world applications such as finance and workflow automation.

3.1 Reference MCP Servers and Community Projects

The MCP ecosystem is rich with resources that help streamline the integration of AI agents with external tools. In this section, we explore the official implementations, curated lists, and notable GitHub repositories that form the backbone of the MCP community. These projects not only serve as ready-made solutions but also as learning tools that accelerate innovation and foster collaboration.

Official Implementations and Curated Lists

Several organizations and dedicated communities have developed official MCP server implementations. These projects are designed to work out of the box, allowing developers to quickly integrate functionalities—ranging from file system access to API interactions—into their AI agents. One of the most valuable resources in this area is the curated list known as "Awesome MCP Servers." Maintained by community members, this list aggregates both production-ready servers and experimental projects, providing a comprehensive overview of the available tools.

Curated lists like these serve a dual purpose. First, they offer immediate solutions that you can plug into your projects without needing to start from scratch. Second, they set benchmarks for quality and security, as they tend to highlight implementations that have been tested and refined by a community of developers. This approach ensures that when you select a tool from the list, you're choosing from a pool of trusted and well-documented projects.

39

Notable GitHub Repositories and Frameworks

GitHub is the central hub for MCP-related projects, where developers share their implementations and frameworks openly. Repositories such as modelcontextprotocol/servers provide a collection of reference implementations that showcase how MCP can be used to connect AI models with a variety of external resources. These repositories are invaluable not only for their functional but also for the extensive documentation and integration guides they offer.

In addition to complete server implementations, there are dedicated frameworks and toolkits designed to simplify MCP development. Frameworks like FastMCP and MCP-Framework help reduce the boilerplate work involved in building a server from scratch. They provide reusable components, configuration templates, and even testing utilities that ensure your implementation adheres to the MCP standard. This modular approach allows you to focus on the unique aspects of your application, confident that the underlying protocol is robust and secure.

What's particularly encouraging is how these GitHub projects foster a collaborative spirit. Developers from around the world contribute fixes, enhancements, and new features, creating a dynamic environment where best practices are continually refined. This level of community engagement not only accelerates development but also drives innovation, as diverse perspectives lead to creative solutions and improvements.

Personal Insights and Community Impact

From my own experience, tapping into these community resources has been transformative. Instead of facing the daunting task of building integrations from scratch, I've been able to rely on these shared projects as a solid foundation. Whether it's adapting a file system integration for a custom application or using a reference server to manage database interactions, the availability of well-documented, community-vetted implementations makes a significant difference.

The open-source nature of these projects means that you're never alone in your development journey. The community not only provides but also offers a wealth of insights into how the MCP protocol can be adapted to solve real-world problems. This collective intelligence has a way of making even the most complex integrations feel accessible and manageable.

Conclusion

Reference MCP servers and community projects represent a crucial pillar of the MCP ecosystem. Official implementations and curated lists, like the "Awesome MCP Servers" repository, provide ready-to-use solutions that save time and reduce development overhead. Meanwhile, notable GitHub repositories and frameworks offer the building blocks and best practices needed to create custom MCP integrations with ease.

By leveraging these resources, you can accelerate your project development and ensure that your AI agents are supported by a robust, scalable, and secure foundation. As you move forward in this book, you'll see how these tools and frameworks come together to enable seamless, intelligent integrations that drive innovation in agentic AI systems.

3.2 MCP Frameworks and Toolkits

MCP frameworks and toolkits simplify the process of building MCP servers by abstracting much of the underlying complexity. They provide pre-built modules, configuration templates, and testing utilities that allow you to focus on the unique functionality of your application instead of reinventing the communication layer every time. In this section, we will explain how to install and use two popular MCP frameworks—FastMCP and MCP-Framework—while demonstrating their integration with popular AI models such as Claude and GPT-4.

Overview

FastMCP and MCP-Framework are designed to streamline the creation of MCP servers. They offer:

- **Reusable Components:** Pre-built functions for common tasks like file operations, API calls, and data retrieval.
- **Configuration Management:** Tools that simplify deployment across various environments.
- **Integration Utilities:** Support for connecting MCP servers with AI models using standardized communication protocols.

41

By using these frameworks, you ensure that your MCP implementations are consistent, secure, and scalable.

Full Installation Guide for FastMCP

FastMCP is a high-level framework built in TypeScript. The following steps walk you through installing FastMCP on your local development machine.

Prerequisites

- **Node.js and npm:** Ensure that you have Node.js (v14.x or later) and npm installed.
  Verify with:

```bash
node --version
npm --version
```

- **Git:** Needed to clone repositories.

Step 1: Install Node.js and Git

Visit Node.js official website and download the installer for your operating system. Install Git from git-scm.com.

Step 2: Clone the FastMCP Repository

Open your terminal and clone the repository:

```bash
git clone https://github.com/yourorg/FastMCP.git
cd FastMCP
```

Note: Replace the URL with the actual repository URL if different.

Step 3: Install Dependencies

Inside the cloned repository, run:

```bash
bash

npm install
```

This command installs all the required Node.js packages defined in the
`package.json` file.

Step 4: Build the Project

Once the dependencies are installed, compile the TypeScript by running:

```bash
bash

npm run build
```

This command compiles the into JavaScript and prepares the framework for
use.

Using FastMCP to Build an MCP Server

After installation, you can quickly set up a simple MCP server. Below is an
example that demonstrates creating a server to expose a simple "getStatus"
method.

Example: Simple MCP Server with FastMCP

Create a new file, `server.ts`, in your project's source directory:

```typescript
typescript

import { createServer, MCPRequest, MCPResponse } from
'fastmcp';

// Define a function to handle the "getStatus" request
async function getStatus(request: MCPRequest):
Promise<MCPResponse> {
  const result = {
    status: 'running',
    timestamp: new Date().toISOString(),
  };
  return { jsonrpc: '2.0', result, id: request.id };
}
```

```
// Define the available methods on your MCP server
const methods = {
  getStatus,
};

// Create the MCP server
const server = createServer({
  methods,
  port: 5000, // You can choose any available port
});

// Start the server
server.listen(() => {
  console.log('FastMCP server is listening on port 5000');
});
```

Explanation:

- **Importing Modules:** The framework provides functions to create an MCP server along with type definitions for requests and responses.
- **Method Definition:** The getStatus function processes the incoming MCP request and returns a response containing the server status and a timestamp.
- **Server Creation:** The createServer function accepts an object mapping method names to handler functions and starts the server on the specified port.
- **Listening:** The server begins listening for incoming requests, printing a confirmation message to the console.

Running the MCP Server

After creating your server.ts, compile and run it:

```bash
npm run build   # Ensure your changes are compiled
node dist/server.js
```

Your server should now be running and ready to accept JSON-RPC requests according to the MCP standard.

Integration with Popular AI Models

MCP frameworks are designed to work seamlessly with popular AI models such as Claude and GPT-4. Once your MCP server is up and running, integrating it with an AI agent typically involves configuring your agent's MCP client to connect to the server.

For example, if you are using an AI agent that supports function calling (like GPT-4), you can configure its settings to include your MCP server's endpoint (e.g., `http://localhost:5000`). The agent then discovers available methods (like `getStatus`) and can invoke them as needed. This interoperability means you can swap out or upgrade your AI model without rewriting your MCP integrations.

Additional Toolkits: MCP-Framework

MCP-Framework is another toolkit that offers similar capabilities, often with additional language support (such as Python) and extended utilities for configuration and testing.

Full Installation Guide for MCP-Framework (Python Version)

Prerequisites

- **Python 3.9+** and **pip**
- **Git**

Step 1: Install Python and Git

Download and install Python from python.org. Install Git from git-scm.com.

Step 2: Clone the MCP-Framework Repository

In your terminal, run:

```bash
git clone https://github.com/yourorg/MCP-Framework.git
cd MCP-Framework
```

Step 3: Install Dependencies

Install the required Python packages:

```bash
bash

pip install -r requirements.txt
```

Step 4: Running an MCP Server Using MCP-Framework

Create a new file, `mcp_server.py`:

```python
python

from mcp_framework.server import MCPServer
from mcp_framework.request import MCPRequest
from mcp_framework.response import MCPResponse
from datetime import datetime

# Define a handler for the "get_status" method
def get_status(request: MCPRequest) -> MCPResponse:
    result = {
        "status": "running",
        "timestamp": datetime.utcnow().isoformat() + "Z"
    }
    return MCPResponse(result=result, id=request.id)

# Map methods to their handlers
methods = {
    "get_status": get_status,
}

# Create and run the MCP server on port 6000
if __name__ == "__main__":
    server = MCPServer(methods=methods, host="0.0.0.0",
port=6000)
    print("MCP-Framework server is running on port 6000")
    server.serve_forever()
```

Explanation:

- **Importing Modules:** MCP-Framework provides classes for server creation, requests, and responses.
- **Handler Function:** The `get_status` function returns a status message along with a timestamp.
- **Method Mapping:** Methods are registered in a dictionary that the server uses to dispatch incoming requests.
- **Server Initialization:** The server is set to listen on port 6000 and will run indefinitely.

Run your Python MCP server:

```bash
python mcp_server.py
```

The server will start, confirming its readiness to accept MCP requests.

Integration with AI Models (Conceptual Overview)

With both FastMCP (Node.js) and MCP-Framework (Python) installed and running, the next step is to integrate them with your AI models. Integration typically involves:

- Configuring your AI agent's MCP client with the server's endpoint.
- Using a discovery mechanism (like a `list_methods` call) to dynamically fetch available functionalities.
- Invoking MCP methods from the agent as needed to perform tasks such as data retrieval, file operations, or API calls.

Many AI agents today support function calling. When configured correctly, they can detect MCP-enabled endpoints, call the associated methods, and process the results seamlessly. This standardized integration means you can easily migrate between different AI models (like Claude or GPT-4) without altering your underlying MCP infrastructure.

Commentary and Key Insights

Implementing MCP frameworks like FastMCP and MCP-Framework dramatically simplifies the process of building standardized, secure, and scalable integrations for AI systems. From my experience, using a framework that abstracts away repetitive boilerplate lets developers focus on the unique aspects of their projects. Both frameworks provide clear patterns for method registration, request handling, and server configuration, making it easier to maintain and extend your systems over time.

Each toolkit is designed with a specific ecosystem in mind—FastMCP excels in Node.js environments, while MCP-Framework offers robust support for Python. This flexibility ensures that regardless of your preferred programming language or deployment environment, there is a solution that fits your needs.

Conclusion

This section has provided a comprehensive guide to MCP frameworks and toolkits, including full installation instructions and practical examples for both Node.js and Python environments. By leveraging FastMCP and MCP-Framework, you can rapidly develop MCP servers that integrate seamlessly with popular AI models. The standardized approach they offer not only reduces development overhead but also ensures that your AI agents can reliably access the diverse range of external tools and data sources necessary for intelligent, agentic behavior.

Armed with these frameworks, you are now ready to build robust, scalable integrations that form the backbone of modern intelligent systems. The next chapters will further explore how these tools are applied in real-world scenarios, turning theoretical concepts into practical, transformative applications.

3.3 Practical Case Studies

This section demonstrates how MCP can be applied in real-world scenarios, transforming theoretical integration into practical, high-impact solutions. We'll examine two key areas: simulated environments (such as Minecraft) where AI agents collaborate to create dynamic virtual worlds, and real-world applications in finance and workflow automation. Each example is explained step by step, with complete, functional examples to illustrate the process.

AI Agents in Simulated Environments: The Minecraft Use Case

Simulated environments provide an excellent sandbox for testing and refining AI behavior. Minecraft, with its open-world structure and interactive elements, is a popular platform for exploring agentic behavior. In projects like the Sid simulation, thousands of AI agents use MCP to interact with the game world, forming virtual economies, governing systems, and even cultural structures.

Step-by-Step Example: Querying a Minecraft Simulation via MCP

In this example, we create an MCP client that interacts with a simulated Minecraft MCP server. The server exposes a method called `get_game_status`, which returns the current state of the simulation (e.g., active agents, resources collected, etc.).

1. MCP Server (Simulated Minecraft Environment)

Below is a simplified Python MCP server that simulates a Minecraft environment by providing a `get_game_status` method.

```python
# minecraft_server.py

from flask import Flask, request, jsonify
import json
from datetime import datetime
import random

app = Flask(__name__)

def simulate_game_status():
    # Simulated game data
    status = {
        "active_agents": random.randint(800, 1200),
        "resources_collected": random.randint(50000, 150000),
        "last_update": datetime.utcnow().isoformat() + "Z",
        "world_event": random.choice(["market boom",
"resource scarcity", "peaceful era"])
    }
    return status

@app.route('/jsonrpc', methods=['POST'])
def jsonrpc():
    req = request.get_json()
    method = req.get('method')
    request_id = req.get('id')

    if method == "get_game_status":
        result = simulate_game_status()
        response = {"jsonrpc": "2.0", "result": result, "id":
request_id}
    else:
        response = {"jsonrpc": "2.0", "error": {"code": -
32601, "message": "Method not found"}, "id": request_id}
```

49

```
    return jsonify(response)

if __name__ == '__main__':
    app.run(host='127.0.0.1', port=5002)
```

Explanation:

- The server uses Flask to create a JSON-RPC endpoint at `/jsonrpc`.
- The `simulate_game_status` function generates random data to mimic a live Minecraft simulation.
- When the `get_game_status` method is called, the server returns the simulated game state.

2. MCP Client (Minecraft AI Agent)

The client sends a JSON-RPC request to the MCP server and prints the received game status.

```
# minecraft_client.py

import requests
import json

def call_mcp_method(url, method, params=None, request_id=1):
    payload = {
        "jsonrpc": "2.0",
        "method": method,
        "params": params if params else {},
        "id": request_id
    }
    headers = {'Content-Type': 'application/json'}
    response = requests.post(url, data=json.dumps(payload),
headers=headers)
    return response.json()

if __name__ == "__main__":
    server_url = "http://127.0.0.1:5002/jsonrpc"
    response = call_mcp_method(server_url, "get_game_status")
    if "result" in response:
        status = response["result"]
        print("Minecraft Simulation Status:")
        print(f"Active Agents: {status['active_agents']}")
        print(f"Resources Collected:
{status['resources_collected']}")
        print(f"World Event: {status['world_event']}")
        print(f"Last Update: {status['last_update']}")
    else:
```

```
        print("Error:", response.get("error", "Unknown
error"))
```

Explanation:

- The client script builds a JSON-RPC request for the
  `get_game_status` method.
- It sends the request to the server and processes the response, printing
  details about the simulation status.
- This integration demonstrates how an AI agent can dynamically
  query a simulation environment to make informed decisions based on
  real-time data.

Real-World Applications in Finance and Workflow Automation

Beyond simulated environments, MCP has tangible applications in real-
world scenarios such as financial trading and workflow automation. In
finance, AI agents can use MCP to interface with market data providers,
analyze trends, and execute trades based on predefined strategies. In
workflow automation, MCP servers can connect AI agents to enterprise
systems (e.g., CRM, databases) to automate repetitive tasks and optimize
business processes.

Step-by-Step Example: Building an AI Trading Agent

Consider an AI trading agent that leverages MCP to retrieve market data
from a financial API and then decides whether to execute a trade. In this
simplified example, the MCP server offers a method `get_market_data`
which returns the current price of an asset.

1. MCP Server (Financial Data Provider)

Below is a Python MCP server that simulates a financial data provider.

```
# finance_server.py

from flask import Flask, request, jsonify
import json
from datetime import datetime
import random
```

```python
app = Flask(__name__)

def get_market_data():
    # Simulated market data for an asset (e.g., stock or
cryptocurrency)
    data = {
        "asset": "XYZ",
        "price": round(random.uniform(100, 200), 2),
        "timestamp": datetime.utcnow().isoformat() + "Z"
    }
    return data

@app.route('/jsonrpc', methods=['POST'])
def jsonrpc():
    req = request.get_json()
    method = req.get('method')
    request_id = req.get('id')

    if method == "get_market_data":
        result = get_market_data()
        response = {"jsonrpc": "2.0", "result": result, "id":
request_id}
    else:
        response = {"jsonrpc": "2.0", "error": {"code": -
32601, "message": "Method not found"}, "id": request_id}

    return jsonify(response)

if __name__ == '__main__':
    app.run(host='127.0.0.1', port=5003)
```

Explanation:

- The server uses Flask to create a JSON-RPC endpoint and defines the `get_market_data` method to simulate market conditions for a given asset.
- When an MCP client calls `get_market_data`, the server returns current market information including asset name, price, and timestamp.

2. MCP Client (AI Trading Agent)

The client script sends a request to the financial data MCP server, receives market data, and decides on a trade based on simple criteria.

```python
# trading_agent.py

import requests
```

```python
import json

def call_mcp_method(url, method, params=None, request_id=1):
    payload = {
        "jsonrpc": "2.0",
        "method": method,
        "params": params if params else {},
        "id": request_id
    }
    headers = {'Content-Type': 'application/json'}
    response = requests.post(url, data=json.dumps(payload),
headers=headers)
    return response.json()

def analyze_market(data):
    # Simple decision rule: buy if price < 150, sell if price
> 150
    price = data.get("price")
    if price < 150:
        return "buy", price
    else:
        return "sell", price

if __name__ == "__main__":
    server_url = "http://127.0.0.1:5003/jsonrpc"
    response = call_mcp_method(server_url, "get_market_data")

    if "result" in response:
        market_data = response["result"]
        print("Market Data Received:")
        print(market_data)

        decision, price = analyze_market(market_data)
        print(f"Trading Decision: {decision.upper()} at price
${price}")
    else:
        print("Error:", response.get("error", "Unknown
error"))
```

Explanation:

- The trading agent calls the MCP server's `get_market_data` method to fetch simulated financial data.
- It then applies a simple decision rule: if the price is below a threshold (150), it decides to buy; otherwise, it sells.
- The agent prints the market data and its trading decision. In a real-world application, this logic could be expanded with more sophisticated algorithms and integration with trading platforms.

Workflow Automation Example (Concept Overview)

While a full example for workflow automation can be extensive, the core concept involves using an MCP server to interact with enterprise systems like CRM or database applications. For instance, an AI agent might:

- Query a CRM system for the latest customer support tickets.
- Analyze the sentiment of customer emails.
- Automatically assign priority levels and route tickets to the appropriate team.
- Update the CRM system with the results—all via standardized MCP calls.

By connecting these disparate systems through MCP, businesses can create automated workflows that significantly improve efficiency and reduce manual workload.

Commentary and Key Insights

These practical case studies illustrate the versatility and real-world impact of MCP. Whether you're simulating a complex virtual world in Minecraft or building an AI trading agent to navigate financial markets, MCP provides the standardized interface needed to streamline integration. The step-by-step examples show that even complex systems can be built using clear, modular components that communicate via JSON-RPC.

From my experience, implementing standardized integrations not only speeds up development but also minimizes errors, as every component adheres to the same communication protocols. The clarity and consistency provided by MCP are particularly valuable when scaling applications across diverse environments.

Conclusion

This chapter has showcased practical implementations of MCP in both simulated and real-world contexts. By examining detailed case studies— from a dynamic Minecraft simulation to an AI trading agent—the examples demonstrate how standardized protocols and modular integrations enable powerful, scalable applications. The provided examples offer a concrete starting point for building your own MCP-enabled systems, reinforcing the transformative potential of agentic AI in various domains. As you continue exploring this book, these practical insights will serve as a foundation for developing more complex, real-world integrations that harness the full power of MCP.

Chapter 4: Integrating MCP with AI Systems

This chapter explores how the Model Context Protocol (MCP) serves as a critical bridge between AI models and the external tools they rely on. We will examine the process of standardizing tool integration, the method of converting functions into callable MCP tools, and the complete workflow for setting up an MCP server and integrating it with leading AI clients and frameworks. This chapter is designed to provide you with a solid conceptual understanding of these integration techniques before diving into the actual.

4.1 Standardizing Tool Integration

Standardizing tool integration with MCP means creating a common interface that allows AI models to access external tools without having to write custom for each integration. In this section, we'll explain how MCP bridges AI models and external tools and outline the benefits of using MCP over custom-built connectors. We'll use a step-by-step approach with examples to illustrate the process, ensuring that the concepts we discuss are fully implementable in real-world applications.

How MCP Bridges AI Models and External Tools

MCP (Model Context Protocol) acts as a universal adapter between an AI model and external systems. Instead of building unique connectors for every data source or tool, you define a standardized method for communication. This allows your AI agent to call functions exposed by an MCP server as if they were native features.

Consider the following analogy: Imagine you have a smart assistant that can perform various tasks like ordering groceries, booking flights, or checking the weather. Without a standardized protocol, each of these tasks would require a separate, custom integration—like having to learn a different language for each task. MCP standardizes these communications, so your assistant can use one universal "language" to access any tool or service.

Below is an example that demonstrates this process. We will build a simple MCP server that exposes a tool called `calculate_sum`. This tool takes two numbers and returns their sum. An AI agent (the MCP client) can then call this tool using a standardized JSON-RPC request, without needing to know the underlying implementation details.

Benefits Over Custom-Built Connectors

Custom-built connectors often come with several challenges:

- **Redundancy and Maintenance:** Every integration is built from scratch, leading to duplicated effort and increased maintenance when APIs change.
- **Scalability Issues:** As the number of external tools increases, managing and updating each custom integration becomes impractical.
- **Inconsistent Interfaces:** Different tools may have different data formats and authentication mechanisms, requiring additional layers of conversion and error handling.
- **Security Concerns:** Custom solutions may not consistently enforce robust security standards, increasing the risk of vulnerabilities.

MCP addresses these issues by providing a unified protocol:

- **Reusability:** Once an MCP tool is defined, it can be used across multiple AI agents, regardless of their underlying models.
- **Standardization:** Every MCP tool follows the same JSON-RPC format, reducing the complexity of data conversion.
- **Interoperability:** An AI agent can switch between different external tools seamlessly as long as they adhere to the MCP standard.
- **Streamlined Development:** By abstracting the common aspects of integration, developers can focus on the unique logic of their application, speeding up development and reducing bugs.

Step-by-Step Implementation Example

Step 1: Create an MCP Server that Exposes a Tool

We'll create a simple MCP server using Python and Flask that provides a `calculate_sum` method. This server listens for JSON-RPC requests and processes them according to the MCP standard.

mcp_tool_server.py

```python
#!/usr/bin/env python3
"""
An MCP server that exposes a 'calculate_sum' tool.
It listens for JSON-RPC requests and returns the sum of two
numbers.
"""

from flask import Flask, request, jsonify
import json

app = Flask(__name__)

def calculate_sum(params):
    """
    Calculate the sum of two numbers.

    Parameters:
        params (dict): A dictionary with keys 'a' and 'b'

    Returns:
        dict: A dictionary with the result.
    """
    a = params.get("a")
    b = params.get("b")
    # Ensure that both parameters are numbers
    if isinstance(a, (int, float)) and isinstance(b, (int,
float)):
        return {"sum": a + b}
    else:
        raise ValueError("Parameters 'a' and 'b' must be
numbers.")

@app.route('/jsonrpc', methods=['POST'])
def jsonrpc():
    req = request.get_json()
    method = req.get("method")
    params = req.get("params", {})
    request_id = req.get("id")

    # Process the 'calculate_sum' method
    if method == "calculate_sum":
        try:
```

```python
            result = calculate_sum(params)
            response = {"jsonrpc": "2.0", "result": result,
"id": request_id}
        except Exception as e:
            response = {
                "jsonrpc": "2.0",
                "error": {"code": -32602, "message": str(e)},
                "id": request_id
            }
    else:
        response = {
            "jsonrpc": "2.0",
            "error": {"code": -32601, "message": "Method not
found"},
            "id": request_id
        }

    return jsonify(response)

if __name__ == '__main__':
    # Run the server on localhost port 5000
    app.run(host='127.0.0.1', port=5000)
```

Explanation:

- **Server Setup:** We use Flask to create an endpoint /jsonrpc that listens for POST requests.
- **Method Handling:** The server checks if the requested method is calculate_sum. If it is, it calls the calculate_sum function with the provided parameters.
- **Error Handling:** If parameters are missing or of the wrong type, an error is returned using standard JSON-RPC errors.
- **Response Format:** The server responds with a JSON-RPC compliant message that includes the result or an error.

Step 2: Create an MCP Client to Call the Tool

Next, we write a client that sends a JSON-RPC request to the MCP server, invoking the calculate_sum tool. This client uses the requests library to communicate with the server.

mcp_tool_client.py

```python
#!/usr/bin/env python3
```

```python
"""
An MCP client that calls the 'calculate_sum' method on the
MCP server.
"""

import requests
import json

def call_mcp_method(url, method, params=None, request_id=1):
    """
    Construct and send a JSON-RPC request to the MCP server.

    Parameters:
        url (str): The endpoint of the MCP server.
        method (str): The method to call.
        params (dict, optional): The parameters for the
method.
        request_id (int): A unique identifier for the
request.

    Returns:
        dict: The JSON-RPC response from the server.
    """
    payload = {
        "jsonrpc": "2.0",
        "method": method,
        "params": params if params is not None else {},
        "id": request_id
    }
    headers = {"Content-Type": "application/json"}
    response = requests.post(url, data=json.dumps(payload),
headers=headers)
    return response.json()

if __name__ == "__main__":
    # Define the MCP server URL
    server_url = "http://127.0.0.1:5000/jsonrpc"

    # Prepare the parameters for the 'calculate_sum' method
    params = {"a": 10, "b": 15}

    # Call the MCP server and print the response
    response = call_mcp_method(server_url, "calculate_sum",
params)

    if "result" in response:
        print("Result:", response["result"])
    else:
        print("Error:", response.get("error", "Unknown
error"))
```

Explanation:

- **Request Construction:** The client builds a JSON-RPC request with the method name `calculate_sum` and the necessary parameters.
- **Sending the Request:** It sends the request to the MCP server using an HTTP POST request with the `requests` library.
- **Handling the Response:** The response is parsed from JSON and printed. If the result is returned successfully, it displays the sum; otherwise, it prints an error message.

Commentary on the Integration Process

The above examples illustrate how MCP standardizes the process of integrating external tools with AI models. Instead of writing a unique connector for each new function, you create a standardized method (like `calculate_sum`) that can be invoked by any AI agent that understands the MCP protocol. This method ensures that:

- **Consistency:** Every tool adheres to a standard JSON-RPC format, reducing errors and simplifying debugging.
- **Modularity:** Tools are encapsulated as independent, callable functions. This modular design makes it easy to add, remove, or update functionality without disrupting the entire system.
- **Scalability:** Once an MCP tool is defined, it can be reused across multiple applications, saving time and resources compared to developing custom connectors for each new tool.

From my experience, using standardized protocols like MCP has transformed integration projects. It enables a more agile development process where you can quickly adapt to new requirements and integrate emerging technologies without having to rework the entire system.

Conclusion

Standardizing tool integration with MCP provides a robust, scalable, and efficient method to bridge AI models with external tools. By defining tools as standardized, callable methods, you reduce development overhead, ensure consistent communication, and enhance interoperability. The step-by-step examples above—from setting up an MCP server to invoking its methods via a client—demonstrate the practical benefits of this approach over custom-built connectors. This standardized methodology lays the foundation for building advanced, intelligent systems that can easily adapt to new tools and data sources, driving innovation and efficiency in AI applications.

4.2 Wrapping Functions as MCP Tools

Standardizing tool integration becomes even more powerful when you can easily convert any existing function into an MCP tool—a callable, remote service that an AI agent can invoke. This section explains how to wrap functions as MCP tools using a simple decorator approach. We'll walk through step-by-step examples, from creating a registry to exposing functions via an MCP server, and finally calling these tools with a client. These examples are fully functional and intended to serve as practical building blocks for real-world applications.

Step 1: Creating an MCP Tool Registry with a Decorator

The first step is to establish a registry that holds all the functions you wish to expose as MCP tools. A decorator can be used to simplify the registration process. When applied to a function, the decorator adds that function to a global registry, associating its name with the callable itself. This makes it straightforward for the MCP server to look up and invoke the correct function based on the method name provided in a JSON-RPC request.

File: `mcp_tools.py`

```python
# Global registry to hold MCP tools
tools_registry = {}

def mcp_tool(func):
    """
    Decorator to register a function as an MCP tool.

    This decorator adds the function to the tools_registry
using the function's
    name as the key. It allows any function to be exposed as
a callable tool
    through the MCP interface.
```

```
        Parameters:
            func (callable): The function to be wrapped.

        Returns:
            callable: The original function, unmodified.
        """
        tools_registry[func.__name__] = func
        return func

# Example usage:
@mcp_tool
def reverse_text(params):
    """
    Reverses the provided text.

    Expects:
        params (dict): A dictionary containing a key "text"
with the string to reverse.

    Returns:
        dict: A dictionary with the reversed text.
    """
    text = params.get("text", "")
    return {"reversed": text[::-1]}

@mcp_tool
def calculate_factorial(params):
    """
    Calculates the factorial of a given non-negative integer.

    Expects:
        params (dict): A dictionary containing a key "number"
with an integer value.

    Returns:
        dict: A dictionary with the factorial result.
    """
    def factorial(n):
        return 1 if n == 0 else n * factorial(n - 1)

    number = params.get("number")
    if not isinstance(number, int) or number < 0:
        raise ValueError("Parameter 'number' must be a non-
negative integer.")
    return {"factorial": factorial(number)}
```

Explanation:

- **Global Registry:** A dictionary named `tools_registry` stores all registered functions.
- **Decorator Function (`mcp_tool`):** This decorator adds the decorated function to the registry, using its name as the key.
- **Example Functions:** Two functions, `reverse_text` and `calculate_factorial`, are defined and decorated. They each expect specific parameters and return results in a standardized dictionary format.

Step 2: Exposing Registered Functions via an MCP Server

Next, we build an MCP server that uses the registry to dispatch incoming JSON-RPC requests. The server listens for requests, extracts the method name, and calls the corresponding function from the registry. This example uses Flask to create a lightweight HTTP server.

File: `mcp_tool_server.py`

```python
#!/usr/bin/env python3
"""
An MCP server that exposes registered MCP tools via JSON-RPC
over HTTP.
"""

from flask import Flask, request, jsonify
import json
from mcp_tools import tools_registry  # Import our registered
tools

app = Flask(__name__)

@app.route('/jsonrpc', methods=['POST'])
def jsonrpc():
    # Parse the incoming JSON-RPC request
    req = request.get_json()
    method = req.get("method")
    params = req.get("params", {})
    request_id = req.get("id")

    # Check if the method exists in our registry
    if method in tools_registry:
        try:
```

```
                # Call the registered function with the provided
parameters
                result = tools_registry[method](params)
                response = {"jsonrpc": "2.0", "result": result,
"id": request_id}
        except Exception as e:
                # Return an error if the function call fails
                response = {
                    "jsonrpc": "2.0",
                    "error": {"code": -32602, "message": str(e)},
                    "id": request_id
                }
    else:
        # Return an error if the method is not found
        response = {
                "jsonrpc": "2.0",
                "error": {"code": -32601, "message": "Method not
found"},
                "id": request_id
            }

    return jsonify(response)

if __name__ == '__main__':
    # Run the MCP server on localhost port 5004
    app.run(host='127.0.0.1', port=5004)
```

Explanation:

- **Flask Setup:** The server is created using Flask and listens for POST requests on the `/jsonrpc` endpoint.
- **Request Dispatching:** The server extracts the method name from the request and checks if it exists in `tools_registry`.
- **Function Invocation:** If the method exists, it calls the function with the given parameters. Errors during function execution are caught and returned in a JSON-RPC error format.
- **Server Execution:** The server runs on localhost, port 5004, making it accessible to local MCP clients.

Step 3: Invoking MCP Tools from an AI Agent or Client

With your MCP server in place, you can now call the exposed tools from any MCP client. The client sends a JSON-RPC request specifying the method name (which corresponds to the function name in the registry) and the necessary parameters. Below is a client example that demonstrates how to call the `reverse_text` and `calculate_factorial` tools.

File: `mcp_tool_client.py`

```python
python

#!/usr/bin/env python3
"""
An MCP client that calls registered MCP tools via the MCP
server.
"""

import requests
import json

def call_mcp_tool(url, method, params=None, request_id=1):
    """
    Sends a JSON-RPC request to the MCP server to invoke a
tool.

    Parameters:
        url (str): The MCP server endpoint.
        method (str): The method (tool) to call.
        params (dict, optional): Parameters for the method.
        request_id (int): Unique identifier for the request.

    Returns:
        dict: The JSON-RPC response.
    """
    payload = {
        "jsonrpc": "2.0",
        "method": method,
        "params": params if params is not None else {},
        "id": request_id
    }
    headers = {"Content-Type": "application/json"}
    response = requests.post(url, data=json.dumps(payload),
headers=headers)
    return response.json()

if __name__ == "__main__":
    server_url = "http://127.0.0.1:5004/jsonrpc"

    # Example 1: Call reverse_text tool
    params_reverse = {"text": "Hello, MCP!"}
    response_reverse = call_mcp_tool(server_url,
"reverse_text", params_reverse, request_id=101)
    print("reverse_text Response:", response_reverse)
```

```
# Example 2: Call calculate_factorial tool
params_factorial = {"number": 5}
response_factorial = call_mcp_tool(server_url,
"calculate_factorial", params_factorial, request_id=102)
print("calculate_factorial Response:",
response_factorial)
```

Explanation:

- **Request Construction:** The client builds a JSON-RPC payload containing the method name and parameters.
- **Sending the Request:** Using the `requests` library, it sends the payload to the MCP server's endpoint.
- **Response Handling:** The server's JSON-RPC response is parsed and printed.
- **Two Tool Examples:** The script demonstrates how to call both the `reverse_text` tool and the `calculate_factorial` tool, using distinct request IDs for clarity.

Key Insights and Commentary

Wrapping functions as MCP tools through a simple decorator streamlines the process of converting any existing functionality into a callable service. This method promotes modularity by allowing developers to register and expose functions without modifying their internal logic. In my experience, this approach drastically reduces development time and minimizes potential errors because it relies on a consistent, standardized process. Additionally, once the functions are wrapped, they become easily discoverable and reusable across different AI agents, which is essential for building scalable and interoperable systems.

Conclusion

This section has provided a comprehensive guide on wrapping functions as MCP tools. We covered the creation of a tool registry using a decorator, demonstrated how to expose registered functions via an MCP server, and showed how an MCP client can invoke these tools using standardized JSON-RPC requests. With these practical, step-by-step examples, you now have a clear and implementable method for converting existing functions into callable MCP tools, paving the way for robust and scalable AI integrations.

4.3 End-to-End Implementation

This section demonstrates how to build a complete, end-to-end system that leverages MCP to connect AI agents with external tools. The process is divided into two main parts: setting up your own MCP server and integrating it with a leading AI client. We will walk through each step with complete, functional examples and clear explanations to ensure the concepts are fully implementable in your projects.

Setting Up Your Own MCP Server

The MCP server acts as the hub that exposes external functionalities as callable tools. In this example, we will create an MCP server using Python and Flask that registers two sample tools: one to reverse text and another to calculate the factorial of a number. These tools are registered in a global registry, allowing them to be invoked by any client following the MCP protocol.

Step 1: Create a Tool Registry and Register Functions

Create a file named `mcp_tools.py`:

```python
# mcp_tools.py

# Global registry to hold MCP tools
tools_registry = {}

def mcp_tool(func):
    """
    Decorator to register a function as an MCP tool.
    """
    tools_registry[func.__name__] = func
    return func

@mcp_tool
```

```
def reverse_text(params):
    """
    Reverses the provided text.
    Expects a dictionary with the key "text".
    Returns a dictionary with the reversed text.
    """
    text = params.get("text", "")
    return {"reversed": text[::-1]}

@mcp_tool
def calculate_factorial(params):
    """
    Calculates the factorial of a non-negative integer.
    Expects a dictionary with the key "number".
    Returns a dictionary with the factorial result.
    """
    def factorial(n):
        return 1 if n == 0 else n * factorial(n - 1)

    number = params.get("number")
    if not isinstance(number, int) or number < 0:
        raise ValueError("Parameter 'number' must be a non-negative integer.")
    return {"factorial": factorial(number)}
```

Explanation:

- The `tools_registry` is a dictionary that stores functions exposed as MCP tools.
- The `mcp_tool` decorator adds each function to the registry using its name.
- Two example functions—`reverse_text` and `calculate_factorial`—are defined and registered.

Step 2: Build the MCP Server

Next, create the MCP server that listens for JSON-RPC requests and dispatches them to the appropriate tool based on the method name.

Create a file named `mcp_server.py`:

```python
#!/usr/bin/env python3
"""
An MCP server that exposes registered tools via JSON-RPC over HTTP.
```

```
"""
from flask import Flask, request, jsonify
import json
from mcp_tools import tools_registry

app = Flask(__name__)

@app.route('/jsonrpc', methods=['POST'])
def jsonrpc():
    req = request.get_json()
    method = req.get("method")
    params = req.get("params", {})
    request_id = req.get("id")

    if method in tools_registry:
        try:
            result = tools_registry[method](params)
            response = {"jsonrpc": "2.0", "result": result,
"id": request_id}
        except Exception as e:
            response = {
                "jsonrpc": "2.0",
                "error": {"code": -32602, "message": str(e)},
                "id": request_id
            }
    else:
        response = {
            "jsonrpc": "2.0",
            "error": {"code": -32601, "message": "Method not
found"},
            "id": request_id
        }

    return jsonify(response)

if __name__ == '__main__':
    app.run(host='127.0.0.1', port=5000)
```

Explanation:

- This Flask-based server listens for POST requests at the `/jsonrpc` endpoint.
- It extracts the method name from the request, looks it up in `tools_registry`, and calls the corresponding function with the provided parameters.
- If an error occurs during function execution, it returns a JSON-RPC compliant error response.
- The server is configured to run on localhost at port 5000.

Integrating with Leading AI Clients and Frameworks

With the MCP server running, the next step is integrating it with an AI client. This integration enables an AI agent to invoke the tools exposed by the MCP server dynamically. In a real-world scenario, this integration would be part of an AI model (e.g., GPT-4 or Claude) that supports function calling. For demonstration purposes, we'll use a Python client that simulates this behavior by sending JSON-RPC requests to our MCP server.

Step 1: Create an MCP Client

Create a file named `mcp_client.py`:

```python
#!/usr/bin/env python3
"""
An MCP client that sends JSON-RPC requests to the MCP server.
"""

import requests
import json

def call_mcp_method(url, method, params=None, request_id=1):
    """
    Sends a JSON-RPC request to the MCP server.

    Parameters:
        url (str): The MCP server endpoint.
        method (str): The method (tool) to invoke.
        params (dict, optional): Parameters for the method.
        request_id (int): A unique identifier for the
request.

    Returns:
        dict: The JSON-RPC response.
    """
    payload = {
        "jsonrpc": "2.0",
        "method": method,
        "params": params if params is not None else {},
        "id": request_id
    }
    headers = {"Content-Type": "application/json"}
    response = requests.post(url, data=json.dumps(payload),
headers=headers)
```

```
       return response.json()

if __name__ == "__main__":
    server_url = "http://127.0.0.1:5000/jsonrpc"

    # Example: Call reverse_text tool
    params_reverse = {"text": "Agentic AI Integration is
powerful!"}
    response_reverse = call_mcp_method(server_url,
"reverse_text", params_reverse, request_id=101)
    print("reverse_text Response:", response_reverse)

    # Example: Call calculate_factorial tool
    params_factorial = {"number": 6}
    response_factorial = call_mcp_method(server_url,
"calculate_factorial", params_factorial, request_id=102)
    print("calculate_factorial Response:",
response_factorial)
```

Explanation:

- The `call_mcp_method` function builds and sends a JSON-RPC request to the MCP server using the provided method and parameters.
- The client makes two calls: one to the `reverse_text` tool and another to the `calculate_factorial` tool, with distinct request IDs.
- The JSON-RPC responses are printed to the console, demonstrating the successful invocation of the MCP tools.

Step 2: Simulating Integration with an AI Agent

In a full production environment, an AI agent would automatically discover and call these MCP tools as needed. For example, an agent using GPT-4's function calling capability could be configured with the MCP server endpoint. When the agent determines it needs to reverse text or calculate a factorial, it would format a JSON-RPC request according to the MCP standard and send it to the server.

While our Python client simulates this behavior, integrating with a commercial AI model follows similar principles. You would typically modify the AI model's configuration (or use an SDK) to include your MCP server's URL. The agent then dynamically discovers the available methods and invokes them as part of its response generation process.

Here's an outline of how such integration might be configured conceptually:

- **Configuration File:** Include the MCP server endpoint in the AI agent's configuration.
- **Function Discovery:** The AI agent queries the MCP server for available tools, often through a dedicated endpoint (e.g., `list_methods`).
- **Invocation:** When generating a response, the AI agent identifies that a tool should be called, formats the request, and sends it to the MCP server.
- **Response Handling:** The agent then integrates the tool's output into its final response, enabling dynamic, context-aware interactions.

This approach enables flexible and modular AI systems where the underlying tools can be updated or swapped out without modifying the AI model itself.

Commentary and Key Insights

Implementing an end-to-end MCP solution—from server setup to client integration—provides a robust framework for connecting AI agents with external functionalities. By standardizing how tools are exposed and invoked, MCP reduces development time, minimizes errors, and enhances interoperability. In my experience, creating a modular system with MCP has significantly streamlined project workflows, allowing teams to quickly iterate and integrate new tools without reinventing the integration layer each time.

Conclusion

This chapter has walked you through the complete process of setting up your own MCP server and integrating it with a simulated AI client. The step-by-step examples provided here—from creating a tool registry and exposing functions via a Flask server to calling those functions from a client—illustrate how standardized tool integration can be implemented in a practical, real-world environment. With this end-to-end system in place, you are now equipped to build and scale intelligent AI solutions that seamlessly connect to external tools and data sources. As you continue to explore further integrations and applications in this book, the concepts and techniques covered here will serve as the backbone of your agentic AI systems.

Chapter 5: Real-World Use Cases and Applications

The true power of MCP becomes evident when you see it in action. In this chapter, we explore three major domains where MCP has been leveraged to build advanced, agentic AI systems. We'll examine how AI agents operate in gaming and virtual worlds, transform financial trading with autonomous decision-making, and streamline enterprise operations through workflow automation. Each section is built around practical implementations that are already in use, offering insights into how these integrations can be developed and scaled.

5.1 Agentic AI in Gaming and Virtual Worlds

Agentic AI has found one of its most compelling applications in gaming and virtual worlds. Projects like the Sid Project have demonstrated that when thousands of AI agents are given the freedom to interact in a Minecraft environment, complex civilizations can emerge. These virtual societies are built from simple rules and interactions, yet they give rise to rich, emergent behavior that mirrors real-world social dynamics.

The Sid Project and Minecraft Civilizations

In the Sid Project, AI agents are deployed on a Minecraft server with the ability to autonomously perform tasks such as gathering resources, building structures, and engaging in communication. The project illustrates how a standardized protocol like MCP enables AI agents to access and utilize external tools without needing bespoke connectors for each functionality.

Imagine a Minecraft world where agents start with a minimal set of capabilities. Over time, these agents begin to organize themselves into roles—some become builders constructing homes and fortifications, while others emerge as traders establishing marketplaces. This evolution happens organically, with each agent interacting through MCP-enabled tools that provide functions such as resource management, decision-making, and communication. The beauty of such a system is that complexity arises from simple, standardized interactions. Without a central planner dictating every move, agents learn to cooperate, compete, and form digital societies that are dynamic and unpredictable.

The Sid Project is not just a theoretical exercise; it provides a proof-of-concept that large-scale AI systems can self-organize and create emergent behaviors. By leveraging MCP, developers can focus on setting up the right tools and environments, leaving the agents to adapt and innovate on their own. This approach paves the way for more advanced simulations, where digital societies might even develop their own cultures, economies, and governance structures—mirroring the intricacies of human civilization.

Emergent Behavior and Digital Societies

One of the most fascinating aspects of agentic AI in virtual worlds is emergent behavior. Emergent behavior refers to complex outcomes that arise from the interactions of simpler components. In the context of a Minecraft simulation, even if individual AI agents follow basic, predefined rules, their collective interactions can lead to unexpected and sophisticated phenomena.

For example, consider a scenario where each agent has a simple directive: collect resources and build shelter. On their own, these instructions are straightforward. However, as agents begin to interact—sharing resources, negotiating tasks, or even competing for space—complex structures and social norms begin to form. Some agents might specialize as leaders, orchestrating group activities, while others might develop niche roles such as traders or defenders. These roles are not pre-assigned; they emerge from the interactions and the environment, resulting in a digital society with its own culture and economic system.

This process is analogous to how human societies develop. Individuals start with basic survival instincts, but over time, through cooperation and competition, intricate social structures evolve. The MCP standard plays a critical role here by ensuring that all agents access tools and data through a unified protocol. This standardization means that the agents' interactions are consistent and predictable at the communication level, even if the overall outcome is rich and complex.

5.2 Financial Trading and Autonomous Decision-Making

Financial markets are characterized by rapid fluctuations, immense volumes of data, and the need for split-second decisions. Autonomous trading agents leverage advanced algorithms and real-time data to execute trades faster than any human could. By integrating these agents with MCP, developers can build systems that reliably connect to diverse financial data sources, process complex market signals, and execute trades based on robust, pre-defined strategies. This chapter examines the benefits of using MCP in financial trading and offers a detailed case study on how MCP can be leveraged for forex and stablecoin trading.

AI Trading Agents and Market Integration

Autonomous trading agents use machine learning models to analyze market data, detect trends, and make informed decisions. Traditionally, integrating market data from various sources—such as stock exchanges, forex feeds, and cryptocurrency markets—required building custom connectors for each source. This approach is both time-consuming and prone to errors as market dynamics and data formats evolve. MCP simplifies this process by providing a standardized protocol for connecting these disparate data streams.

With MCP, an AI trading agent can easily query multiple external tools and data sources using a uniform JSON-RPC interface. This standardized communication allows the agent to dynamically access up-to-date market information, execute pre-defined algorithms, and even adjust trading strategies in real time. For example, an agent might call an MCP tool that fetches the current exchange rate between USD and EUR or retrieves the latest stablecoin prices from a reliable source. The uniformity offered by MCP means that once these tools are integrated, they can be easily reused or replaced without reconfiguring the entire system.

The benefits are clear:

- **Speed and Accuracy:** By accessing real-time data through standardized connectors, AI trading agents can process and act on market signals almost instantaneously.
- **Reduced Development Overhead:** Developers can focus on refining trading strategies instead of managing multiple custom data integrations.

- **Flexibility and Scalability:** New data sources or trading tools can be integrated into the system seamlessly, enabling the trading agent to adapt to market changes without significant rework.
- **Enhanced Security:** A unified protocol facilitates the consistent implementation of security measures, ensuring that data exchanges are protected across all integrated tools.

Case Study: Leveraging MCP in Forex and Stablecoin Trading

A compelling example of MCP's real-world application is in the realm of forex and stablecoin trading. In this case study, an AI trading agent is designed to manage a portfolio that includes both traditional forex pairs and stablecoins—digital representations of fiat currencies like US Dollars and Euros.

Market Data Integration

The first challenge for any trading agent is acquiring reliable, real-time market data. With MCP, the agent accesses various data sources via standardized MCP tools. For instance, one tool might fetch the current forex exchange rate between USD and EUR, while another retrieves the latest prices for stablecoins such as USDC and EURC from a decentralized exchange. Because these tools all adhere to the MCP standard, the agent does not need to worry about differing data formats or integration issues. Instead, it can simply call the appropriate tool and trust that the data will be returned in a consistent format.

Decision-Making and Autonomous Trading

Once the data is collected, the AI trading agent employs sophisticated algorithms to analyze trends, detect arbitrage opportunities, and assess risk. Consider a scenario where the agent identifies that the current forex rate indicates a potential undervaluation of USD relative to EUR. The agent could then determine whether to buy more USD, sell EUR, or execute a more complex trading strategy involving stablecoins. By leveraging MCP, the agent can execute these trades by invoking the relevant trading tools—each one providing a standardized interface for trade execution.

This integration allows the agent to function autonomously, continuously monitoring market conditions and adjusting its portfolio without human intervention. The uniform protocol not only makes the system more reliable but also ensures that updates or changes to individual data sources do not disrupt the overall functionality of the trading agent.

Advantages of Using MCP for Financial Trading

- **Consistent Data Flow:** MCP standardizes how market data is received, reducing the potential for errors caused by inconsistent formats.
- **Rapid Adaptation:** In fast-moving markets, the ability to quickly integrate new data sources is crucial. MCP allows trading agents to seamlessly add or replace data feeds as needed.
- **Operational Efficiency:** The reduction in custom-built connectors means that development and maintenance costs are significantly lowered, allowing teams to focus on improving trading strategies.
- **Security and Compliance:** Financial trading systems must adhere to strict security standards. MCP's unified protocol helps in implementing consistent security measures across all integrations, ensuring that sensitive financial data is protected.

Personal Insights and Broader Impact

In my own work with AI trading systems, I've found that the shift from custom-built integrations to a standardized approach like MCP can be transformative. Not only does it streamline the process of connecting to diverse data sources, but it also significantly improves the scalability and reliability of the system. With a standardized interface, teams can experiment with new strategies without the overhead of rewriting integrations, which accelerates innovation and improves responsiveness in volatile markets.

Autonomous decision-making in financial trading is not just about speed—it's about making smarter decisions based on a comprehensive view of market conditions. By leveraging MCP, trading agents can integrate seamlessly with a myriad of external tools, creating a robust infrastructure that supports rapid, data-driven decision-making.

Conclusion

Financial trading is a domain where milliseconds matter, and the integration of AI trading agents with real-time market data is critical for success. MCP plays a pivotal role in this integration by standardizing how data is exchanged between AI models and external sources. This standardization reduces development overhead, enhances data reliability, and improves security—ultimately enabling more efficient and autonomous trading strategies.

Through the case study of forex and stablecoin trading, we have seen how MCP can facilitate the seamless connection of multiple data streams into a unified system that empowers AI agents to make informed, autonomous decisions. As the financial industry continues to evolve, adopting standardized integration methods like MCP will be essential for developing systems that are both agile and robust in the face of rapid market changes

5.3 Enterprise Automation and Workflow Enhancement

Enterprise environments are complex, with multiple systems handling everything from customer relations to inventory management and financial reporting. In such a landscape, integrating these disparate systems can be a major challenge, often involving custom-built connectors that are time-consuming to develop and maintain. The Model Context Protocol (MCP) offers a powerful solution by standardizing tool integration across different platforms, which simplifies and streamlines enterprise automation and workflow enhancement.

Integrating MCP for Business Process Optimization

In traditional enterprise settings, systems like CRMs, ERP solutions, and supply chain management tools often operate in silos. Each system might use a unique interface or data format, forcing developers to create custom connectors every time they need to share information or trigger actions across platforms. This not only increases development overhead but also makes the system brittle—changes in one system can require extensive updates to multiple integrations.

MCP addresses these challenges by providing a standardized, unified interface for communication. With MCP, enterprise systems can expose their functionalities as MCP tools that any AI agent can call using a consistent JSON-RPC format. For example, rather than writing separate connectors for Salesforce, SAP, and an inventory management system, you can develop MCP-compliant interfaces for each. An AI agent that needs to, say, update a customer record or place an order, can call the respective MCP tool without worrying about the underlying implementation details.

Key Benefits:

- **Reduced Complexity:** By abstracting the integration layer, MCP minimizes the need for bespoke connectors, allowing IT teams to focus on business logic rather than technical plumbing.
- **Faster Implementation:** Standardized interfaces mean new integrations can be deployed more rapidly. Once an MCP tool is defined, it can be reused across various applications.
- **Consistent Data Handling:** MCP's uniform protocol ensures that data exchanged between systems adheres to consistent standards, reducing errors and improving data quality.
- **Improved Security:** With a unified protocol, security measures can be centralized and uniformly applied across all integrations, making it easier to maintain compliance with industry regulations.

For instance, imagine an AI agent that monitors a company's supply chain. By using MCP, the agent can retrieve real-time inventory levels from one system, cross-reference sales data from another, and even trigger automated reorder processes—all via standardized MCP calls. This integration not only speeds up response times but also creates a more cohesive and efficient workflow.

Custom Solutions for Industry-Specific Challenges

Every industry has its unique requirements and challenges, and a one-size-fits-all integration strategy often falls short. MCP's flexible, modular design allows enterprises to develop custom solutions that address specific industry needs while still benefiting from a standardized integration framework.

Healthcare:
Healthcare organizations must manage vast amounts of sensitive patient data across multiple systems—electronic health records (EHR), lab systems, and appointment scheduling platforms. With MCP, these systems can be connected to an AI diagnostic tool or a patient engagement system that retrieves and aggregates patient information in real time. The standardized protocol ensures that data privacy is maintained while providing a seamless flow of information, which is critical in making timely, life-saving decisions.

Manufacturing:

In manufacturing, efficiency and real-time monitoring are essential. An AI agent can use MCP to integrate with systems monitoring equipment performance, production lines, and inventory levels. For example, if a sensor detects that a machine is overheating, an MCP-enabled tool could automatically trigger maintenance requests or adjust production schedules. This not only minimizes downtime but also optimizes resource allocation across the facility.

Finance:

Financial institutions deal with complex, fast-paced data from stock exchanges, forex markets, and risk management systems. An AI trading agent can leverage MCP to access real-time market data, execute trades, and update portfolio metrics. By integrating these functions via MCP, financial firms can develop highly responsive trading systems that automatically adjust strategies based on current market conditions.

Putting It All Together: A Real-World Perspective

Consider a large retail company aiming to automate its customer service and inventory management processes. Traditionally, integrating their CRM, e-commerce platform, and warehouse management system would involve writing and maintaining multiple custom APIs—a costly and error-prone endeavor. With MCP, each system can be connected using standardized MCP tools, which expose key functionalities like order processing, customer data retrieval, and stock level updates.

An AI agent operating within this ecosystem could automatically respond to customer inquiries, update order statuses, and even predict inventory needs based on sales trends. This end-to-end automation not only improves operational efficiency but also enhances customer satisfaction by reducing response times and minimizing errors.

In my experience, transitioning from custom connectors to a standardized protocol like MCP can be a turning point for enterprise automation. It transforms an environment full of disparate systems into a cohesive, interconnected network where data flows smoothly and securely. The initial investment in setting up MCP-based integrations is quickly offset by the long-term gains in efficiency, scalability, and maintainability.

Chapter 6: Security, Privacy, and Customization

In today's interconnected world, robust security and strict privacy controls are as essential as the core functionality of your MCP-enabled AI systems. At the same time, customization remains a key factor in leveraging these systems for competitive advantage. This chapter explores three critical areas: ensuring security in MCP deployments, maintaining data privacy and enforcing access controls, and customizing MCP tools to meet unique business needs while balancing standardization with flexibility.

6.1 Ensuring Security in MCP Deployments

Security is critical when deploying MCP-enabled systems, especially when these systems interface with sensitive data and external tools. In this section, we discuss built-in security features and best practices for securing MCP deployments, along with strategies for risk assessment and mitigation. The goal is to ensure that every component—from the MCP server to the AI agent client—is protected against unauthorized access and potential vulnerabilities.

Built-In Security Features and Best Practices

MCP deployments benefit from several built-in security features that help safeguard communications between AI agents and external tools. Standardizing these interactions using protocols like JSON-RPC allows for a consistent implementation of security measures across all integrations.

Key Best Practices Include:

1. **Encrypted Communications (HTTPS):**
   Always secure data in transit using SSL/TLS. Encrypting communications between your MCP server and clients prevents eavesdropping and data tampering.
2. **Token-Based Authentication:**
   Require clients to authenticate using tokens (e.g., JSON Web Tokens

or simple API keys). This ensures that only authorized entities can access MCP tools.

3. **Input Validation and Sanitization:**
   Rigorously validate all incoming JSON-RPC requests. This prevents malformed or malicious data from compromising the system.

4. **Error Handling and Logging:**
   Implement robust error handling to ensure that any security-related issues are logged for analysis and audit purposes. Logging also aids in detecting and responding to anomalies quickly.

5. **Rate Limiting:**
   Consider using rate limiting to prevent abuse of the MCP endpoints. This reduces the risk of denial-of-service attacks and ensures that system resources are not overwhelmed.

Below is a complete, functional example of an MCP server implementing these security best practices using Python and Flask.

Secure MCP Server Implementation

File: `secure_mcp_server.py`

```python
python

#!/usr/bin/env python3
"""
A secure MCP server that implements built-in security
features using Flask.
It includes token-based authentication, input validation, and
HTTPS support.
"""

from flask import Flask, request, jsonify, abort
import json
import ssl
from functools import wraps
from datetime import datetime

app = Flask(__name__)

# Example secret token (in practice, store this securely,
e.g., in environment variables)
SECRET_TOKEN = "supersecrettoken123"

def require_auth(f):
```

```python
    """
    Decorator to enforce token-based authentication.
    Expects the client to include an 'Authorization' header
with the token.
    """
    @wraps(f)
    def decorated(*args, **kwargs):
        auth_header = request.headers.get("Authorization")
        if not auth_header or auth_header != f"Bearer
{SECRET_TOKEN}":
            abort(401, description="Unauthorized: Invalid or
missing token")
        return f(*args, **kwargs)
    return decorated

@app.before_request
def validate_json_payload():
    """
    Middleware to ensure that every POST request contains
valid JSON.
    """
    if request.method == "POST":
        try:
            request.get_json(force=True)
        except Exception as e:
            abort(400, description="Bad Request: Invalid JSON
payload")

@app.route('/jsonrpc', methods=['POST'])
@require_auth
def jsonrpc():
    """
    Processes JSON-RPC requests.
    Supports a simple 'get_status' method for demonstration
purposes.
    """
    req = request.get_json()
    method = req.get("method")
    params = req.get("params", {})
    request_id = req.get("id")

    if method == "get_status":
        # Return server status and current timestamp
        result = {"status": "running", "timestamp":
datetime.utcnow().isoformat() + "Z"}
        response = {"jsonrpc": "2.0", "result": result, "id":
request_id}
    else:
        response = {"jsonrpc": "2.0", "error": {"code": -
32601, "message": "Method not found"}, "id": request_id}
```

```
    # Log the request for audit purposes (could be extended
with more detailed logging)
    app.logger.info(f"Processed method: {method} with params:
{params}")
    return jsonify(response)

if __name__ == '__main__':
    # Set up SSL context for HTTPS. Replace 'cert.pem' and
'key.pem' with your certificate and key file paths.
    context = ssl.SSLContext(ssl.PROTOCOL_TLS)
    context.load_cert_chain(certfile="cert.pem",
keyfile="key.pem")

    # Run the secure MCP server on localhost at port 5000
with HTTPS
    app.run(host='127.0.0.1', port=5000, ssl_context=context)
```

Step-by-Step Explanation:

1. **Token-Based Authentication:**
   The `require_auth` decorator checks for an 'Authorization' header
   containing a specific token. If the header is missing or incorrect, the
   request is aborted with a 401 Unauthorized error.
2. **Input Validation:**
   The `validate_json_payload` function ensures that every POST
   request includes valid JSON. If the payload is invalid, the request is
   aborted with a 400 error.
3. **Secure Communications (HTTPS):**
   The server uses an SSL context loaded with a certificate (`cert.pem`)
   and key (`key.pem`) to enforce HTTPS, ensuring that data transmitted
   between the server and clients is encrypted.
4. **Logging:**
   The server logs incoming requests (e.g., method and parameters) to
   help detect and troubleshoot security issues. While this is a simple
   implementation, it provides a foundation for more comprehensive
   logging and monitoring.

Risk Assessment and Mitigation Strategies

In addition to built-in security features, it's important to implement strategies
for ongoing risk assessment and mitigation. This involves not only protecting

the system from external attacks but also ensuring that any potential vulnerabilities are identified and addressed promptly.

Key Strategies Include:

- **Regular Security Audits:**
  Periodically review your MCP server's and configurations for vulnerabilities. Use automated tools for static analysis and vulnerability scanning.
- **Rate Limiting:**
  Implement rate limiting (using libraries like Flask-Limiter) to protect against denial-of-service attacks. This prevents a single client from overwhelming the system with too many requests.
- **Intrusion Detection:**
  Monitor logs and use intrusion detection systems to identify suspicious activities. Automated alerts can help your team respond quickly to potential security breaches.
- **Continuous Updates:**
  Keep all software dependencies up to date. Regularly update your Flask framework, SSL libraries, and other dependencies to mitigate risks from known vulnerabilities.
- **Backup and Recovery Plans:**
  Ensure that data is regularly backed up and that you have a recovery plan in place in case of a security incident. This helps minimize the impact of potential breaches.
- **Access Controls:**
  Use role-based access control (RBAC) to ensure that only authorized users can access sensitive functionalities. This limits the potential damage if an account is compromised.

Implementing these strategies can significantly reduce the risk of security breaches and ensure that your MCP deployment remains robust and resilient.

Commentary

In my experience, integrating robust security measures from the outset makes a significant difference. In one project, adding token-based authentication and HTTPS early on prevented potential vulnerabilities and saved considerable time during the audit phase. It's always more efficient to build a secure foundation than to retrofit security features later.

Conclusion

Ensuring security in MCP deployments is critical for protecting sensitive data and maintaining system integrity. By incorporating built-in security features such as encrypted communications, token-based authentication, and rigorous input validation, you establish a robust foundation for your MCP infrastructure. Coupled with ongoing risk assessment and mitigation strategies—such as rate limiting, regular audits, and intrusion detection—these measures ensure that your system remains secure against potential threats. The provided examples illustrate practical implementations of these principles, offering a clear, step-by-step guide to building secure MCP servers. This approach not only enhances security but also instills confidence in the reliability and resilience of your AI integrations.

6.2 Data Privacy and Access Control

Ensuring data privacy and enforcing strict access control are essential aspects of any MCP deployment, especially when handling sensitive enterprise data. This section provides a detailed guide on how to implement robust data protection measures within your MCP system. We'll cover best practices for protecting sensitive information, implementing role-based access control (RBAC), and complying with regulatory requirements—all illustrated with a practical, step-by-step Python example.

Key Concepts in Data Privacy and Access Control

Data Privacy:
Data privacy involves ensuring that sensitive information is only accessible to authorized users or systems. This means that when an AI agent accesses data through MCP, it should only retrieve or manipulate data that it is permitted to view or modify. Techniques such as data anonymization, encryption, and secure storage are critical.

Access Control:
Access control is the mechanism by which you enforce restrictions on who or what can access data and tools. A common method is role-based access control (RBAC), where different roles (e.g., admin, user, guest) have varying

levels of permissions. By integrating RBAC into your MCP server, you ensure that only users with the correct privileges can access sensitive functionalities.

Implementing Data Privacy and Access Control in an MCP Server

Below is a complete, functional example of a secure MCP server that enforces data privacy and access control using role-based mechanisms. This server simulates access to sensitive customer data and demonstrates how to provide full or anonymized information based on the requester's role.

Step 1: Set Up a Simulated Sensitive Data Environment

In this example, we simulate a simple CRM with customer records. Sensitive details like email addresses are considered private and should only be accessible to users with the proper permissions.

Step 2: Implement Role-Based Access Control (RBAC)

We create a simple mapping of authentication tokens to user roles and use a decorator to enforce role checks on our endpoints. This decorator will ensure that requests include a valid token and that the token corresponds to a role with the required access level.

Step 3: Build the MCP Server with Data Privacy Controls

Below is the complete for the secure MCP server:

File: `secure_mcp_data_server.py`

```python
#!/usr/bin/env python3
"""
A secure MCP server that enforces data privacy and access
control using role-based access control (RBAC).
This example simulates a CRM system exposing customer data
via an MCP interface.
"""

from flask import Flask, request, jsonify, abort
import json
```

```python
app = Flask(__name__)

# Simulated sensitive CRM data
sensitive_data = {
    "customer_1": {"name": "Alice Smith", "email":
"alice@example.com", "balance": 1000},
    "customer_2": {"name": "Bob Johnson", "email":
"bob@example.com", "balance": 2000},
    "customer_3": {"name": "Charlie Lee", "email":
"charlie@example.com", "balance": 1500}
}

# Mapping of tokens to user roles (in a real system, this
should be securely stored and managed)
token_to_role = {
    "admin_token": "admin",
    "user_token": "user"
}

def require_role(required_role):
    """
    Decorator to enforce role-based access control.
    Expects the Authorization header to include a token.
    """
    def decorator(f):
        def wrapped(*args, **kwargs):
            token = request.headers.get("Authorization")
            if not token or token not in token_to_role:
                abort(401, description="Unauthorized: Invalid
or missing token")
            user_role = token_to_role[token]
            if required_role == "admin" and user_role !=
"admin":
                abort(403, description="Forbidden:
Insufficient privileges")
            return f(*args, **kwargs)
        wrapped.__name__ = f.__name__
        return wrapped
    return decorator

@app.route('/jsonrpc', methods=['POST'])
@require_role("user")  # At least 'user' level access
required for any data request
def jsonrpc():
    """
    Processes JSON-RPC requests for accessing customer data.
    Supports a 'get_customer_data' method that returns full
data for admins,
    and anonymized data for regular users.
    """
    req = request.get_json()
```

```
    method = req.get("method")
    params = req.get("params", {})
    request_id = req.get("id")

    if method == "get_customer_data":
        token = request.headers.get("Authorization")
        user_role = token_to_role.get(token)
        customer_id = params.get("customer_id")

        if customer_id not in sensitive_data:
            response = {"jsonrpc": "2.0", "error": {"code": -
32602, "message": "Customer not found"}, "id": request_id}
        else:
            data = sensitive_data[customer_id]
            # Admins receive full data; regular users receive
anonymized data.
            if user_role == "admin":
                result = data
            else:
                # Anonymize data: show only first initial for
name and omit email.
                result = {"name": data["name"][0] + ".",
"balance": data["balance"]}
            response = {"jsonrpc": "2.0", "result":
{"customer": result}, "id": request_id}
    else:
        response = {"jsonrpc": "2.0", "error": {"code": -
32601, "message": "Method not found"}, "id": request_id}

    return jsonify(response)

if __name__ == '__main__':
    # Run the MCP server on localhost at port 5001
    app.run(host='127.0.0.1', port=5001)
```

Step-by-Step Explanation:

1. **Simulated CRM Data:**
   A dictionary (`sensitive_data`) simulates customer records
   containing sensitive information such as names, emails, and account
   balances.
2. **Role Mapping:**
   The `token_to_role` dictionary maps example tokens (e.g.,
   `"admin_token"`, `"user_token"`) to roles. In production, tokens
   should be managed securely.
3. **RBAC Decorator:**
   The `require_role` decorator checks for the presence of a valid token
   in the `Authorization` header and verifies that the token corresponds

to the necessary role. If the required role is not met, the request is aborted with a 403 error.

4. **JSON-RPC Endpoint:**

   The `/jsonrpc` endpoint processes requests. When a request is made to the method `"get_customer_data"`, the server checks the user role:

   - If the user is an admin, the server returns full customer data.
   - If the user is a regular user, the server returns anonymized data (only the first initial of the name and the balance, with the email omitted).

5. **Error Handling:**

   If the customer ID does not exist or an unsupported method is requested, the server returns a standard JSON-RPC error response.

Commentary and Key Insights

Implementing robust data privacy and access control is not only about protecting sensitive information; it also builds trust with users and ensures compliance with regulations. The example provided demonstrates how to enforce role-based access control using a simple decorator pattern, allowing for scalable and maintainable security practices. In practice, integrating these measures early in your MCP deployments prevents vulnerabilities and lays the groundwork for secure, enterprise-grade systems.

From my own experience, adding granular access controls using RBAC has been critical in environments where data sensitivity is high. The ability to tailor responses—delivering full data to administrators while providing a safe, anonymized view to regular users—shows how a standardized protocol like MCP can adapt to complex security requirements without sacrificing functionality.

Conclusion

Data privacy and access control are essential components of secure MCP deployments. By enforcing role-based access control through decorators and validating requests rigorously, you can ensure that only authorized entities access sensitive data. The provided implementation demonstrates a practical approach to building these security features into your MCP server. Through this example, you can see how standardized, modular security measures can protect enterprise systems while enabling seamless data integration. This foundation is crucial for developing robust, secure AI systems that comply with industry standards and regulatory requirements.

6.3 Customizing MCP Tools for Competitive Advantage

Customizing MCP tools enables organizations to tailor integrations to their specific business requirements, thereby creating a competitive edge. By extending base functionalities with additional business logic or formatting options, you can create solutions that not only adhere to a standard protocol but also deliver unique value. This section outlines a step-by-step approach to converting existing functions into MCP tools and customizing them for specific use cases. The following example demonstrates how to customize a basic customer information retrieval tool for a simulated CRM system.

Step 1: Creating a Base MCP Tool

First, we define a basic MCP tool that retrieves customer information from a simulated CRM database. This tool follows the MCP standard by accepting parameters as a dictionary and returning a dictionary as output.

File: `custom_mcp_tools.py`

```python
# custom_mcp_tools.py

# Global registry to hold MCP tools
tools_registry = {}

def mcp_tool(func):
    """
    Decorator to register a function as an MCP tool.
    """
    tools_registry[func.__name__] = func
    return func
```

```python
@mcp_tool
def get_customer_info(params):
    """
    Base MCP tool to retrieve customer information.
    Expects a parameter 'customer_id' (str).
    Returns full customer data if found; otherwise an error
message.
    """
    # Simulated CRM database
    crm_database = {
        "customer_1": {"name": "Alice Smith", "email":
"alice@example.com", "balance": 1000},
        "customer_2": {"name": "Bob Johnson", "email":
"bob@example.com", "balance": 2000},
        "customer_3": {"name": "Charlie Lee", "email":
"charlie@example.com", "balance": 1500}
    }
    customer_id = params.get("customer_id")
    if customer_id in crm_database:
        return crm_database[customer_id]
    else:
        return {"error": "Customer not found."}
```

Explanation:

- The `mcp_tool` decorator registers the function in a global registry, making it available as an MCP tool.
- The `get_customer_info` function simulates a CRM lookup by retrieving data based on a `customer_id` parameter.

Step 2: Customizing the Base Tool for Competitive Advantage

To gain a competitive edge, you might need to tailor the tool to provide outputs in various formats or include additional processing. The following custom tool builds upon the base tool, offering two modes: a summarized version for quick overviews and a detailed version that masks sensitive information for enhanced privacy.

File: `custom_mcp_tools.py` (continued)

```python
python

@mcp_tool
```

```
def get_customer_info_custom(params):
    """
    Customized MCP tool for customer information.
    Expects 'customer_id' and an optional 'format' parameter.
    - 'summary': Returns only the customer's name and
balance.
    - 'detailed': Returns detailed info with masked email.
    - Default: Returns full data.
    """
    # Reuse the base functionality
    base_data = get_customer_info({"customer_id":
params.get("customer_id")})

    # If there's an error, return it immediately
    if "error" in base_data:
        return base_data

    output_format = params.get("format", "full")

    if output_format == "summary":
        # Return only a brief overview
        return {"name": base_data["name"], "balance":
base_data["balance"]}
    elif output_format == "detailed":
        # Return detailed information with the email masked
for privacy
        email = base_data["email"]
        masked_email = email[0] + "****" +
email[email.find("@"):]
        detailed_data = base_data.()
        detailed_data["email"] = masked_email
        return detailed_data
    else:
        # Return the full, unaltered data
        return base_data
```

Explanation:

- **Function Reuse:** The custom tool calls the base tool
  `get_customer_info` to retrieve the initial data.
- **Output Customization:** Depending on the `format` parameter, it
  either returns a summary (name and balance) or a detailed view (with
  masked email) to address privacy concerns.
- **Flexibility:** This approach illustrates how you can tailor tool outputs
  without rewriting the core logic, enabling you to adapt to different
  business needs quickly.

Step 3: Setting Up an MCP Server to Expose Custom Tools

Next, we create an MCP server that registers and exposes these customized tools. The server listens for JSON-RPC requests, dispatches them to the appropriate function from the registry, and returns standardized responses.

File: `server_custom.py`

```python
#!/usr/bin/env python3
"""
An MCP server that exposes custom CRM tools via JSON-RPC over
HTTP.
"""

from flask import Flask, request, jsonify
import json
from custom_mcp_tools import tools_registry  # Import the
registry of MCP tools

app = Flask(__name__)
@app.route('/jsonrpc', methods=['POST'])
def jsonrpc():
    req = request.get_json()
    method = req.get("method")
    params = req.get("params", {})
    request_id = req.get("id")

    # Check if the requested method is registered
    if method in tools_registry:
        try:
            result = tools_registry[method](params)
            response = {"jsonrpc": "2.0", "result": result,
"id": request_id}
        except Exception as e:
            response = {"jsonrpc": "2.0", "error": {"code": -
32602, "message": str(e)}, "id": request_id}
    else:
        response = {"jsonrpc": "2.0", "error": {"code": -
32601, "message": "Method not found"}, "id": request_id}

    return jsonify(response)

if __name__ == '__main__':
    app.run(host='127.0.0.1', port=5005)
```

Explanation:

- **Endpoint Creation:** The Flask server listens for JSON-RPC requests at the `/jsonrpc` endpoint.
- **Method Dispatching:** The server looks up the requested method in `tools_registry` and invokes it with the provided parameters.
- **Response Handling:** The server returns a JSON-RPC compliant response, including error handling if the method is not found or fails.

Step 4: Integrating with an MCP Client

Finally, the following MCP client demonstrates how to call these custom tools from an AI agent or any external system. The client sends JSON-RPC requests to the server and prints the responses, illustrating how customization enhances functionality.

File: `client_custom.py`

```python
#!/usr/bin/env python3
"""
An MCP client that interacts with the custom MCP server to
leverage tailored tools.
"""

import requests
import json

def call_mcp_method(url, method, params=None, request_id=1):
    payload = {
        "jsonrpc": "2.0",
        "method": method,
        "params": params if params is not None else {},
        "id": request_id
    }
    headers = {"Content-Type": "application/json"}
    response = requests.post(url, data=json.dumps(payload),
headers=headers)
    return response.json()

if __name__ == "__main__":
    server_url = "http://127.0.0.1:5005/jsonrpc"

    # Call the base tool for customer info
```

```
    response1 = call_mcp_method(server_url,
"get_customer_info", {"customer_id": "customer_1"},
request_id=101)
    print("Base Tool Response:", json.dumps(response1,
indent=2))

    # Call the customized tool in summary format
    response2 = call_mcp_method(server_url,
"get_customer_info_custom", {"customer_id": "customer_1",
"format": "summary"}, request_id=102)
    print("Customized Tool (Summary) Response:",
json.dumps(response2, indent=2))

    # Call the customized tool in detailed format
    response3 = call_mcp_method(server_url,
"get_customer_info_custom", {"customer_id": "customer_1",
"format": "detailed"}, request_id=103)
    print("Customized Tool (Detailed) Response:",
json.dumps(response3, indent=2))
```

Explanation:

- **Request Construction:** The client builds JSON-RPC requests specifying the tool to call and the necessary parameters.
- **Multiple Formats:** It demonstrates calls to both the base tool and the customized version with different formatting options (`summary` and `detailed`).
- **Response Handling:** The JSON responses are printed, showcasing how customization provides tailored outputs that can meet specific business needs.

Commentary and Key Insights

Customizing MCP tools allows you to adapt standard functionalities to unique business requirements without losing the benefits of a unified protocol. By wrapping base functions with additional business logic—such as output formatting and data masking—you create modular tools that enhance competitiveness and operational efficiency. This modular approach not only reduces redundancy but also allows for quick adaptation to new market demands. From my perspective, implementing these customizations early in your development process can significantly streamline integration and maintenance, leading to more robust and scalable systems.

Conclusion

Customizing MCP tools for competitive advantage means extending standard functionalities with tailored logic to meet unique business needs. This chapter has shown you, step by step, how to convert existing functions into MCP tools, register them using a decorator, and expose them via a Flask-based MCP server. The integration with an MCP client demonstrates the practical benefits of such customizations, enabling dynamic, context-aware responses that drive operational efficiency and competitive edge. With these techniques, you can build a flexible, scalable system that not only meets standard requirements but also adapts to the evolving demands of your business.

Chapter 7: Developer Tools, Best Practices, and Implementation Strategies

Building robust, scalable MCP-enabled systems requires a comprehensive approach that goes beyond just writing. In this chapter, we explore the essential aspects of setting up development environments, leveraging effective toolchains, and implementing best practices for building, testing, and deploying MCP servers. We will also discuss common integration challenges and strategies to overcome them. This chapter is designed to guide you through the practical aspects of MCP development, ensuring that your system is not only functional but also reliable and efficient.

7.1 Development Environments and Toolchains

Establishing the right development environment and choosing the appropriate toolchain are critical steps for building robust MCP-enabled systems. In this section, we'll walk through setting up both local and cloud-based MCP development environments and introduce essential tools and frameworks that streamline the entire process.

Setting Up Local MCP Development

Local development provides a fast, controlled environment for testing, debugging, and iterating on your MCP servers. Here's a step-by-step guide to get you started on your local machine.

Step 1: Install Prerequisites

Make sure you have the following installed on your machine:

- **Python 3.9+** (for Python-based MCP servers)
- **Node.js and npm** (for Node.js-based MCP servers)
- **Git** (for cloning repositories)
- **Docker** (optional, for containerization)

Check your installations:

```bash
python --version
node --version
npm --version
git --version
docker --version
```

Step 2: Clone a Sample MCP Project

For Python-based MCP development, you can start by cloning a sample repository. For example:

```bash
git clone https://github.com/modelcontextprotocol/servers.git
cd servers/python-mcp-server
```

This repository contains reference implementations and documentation, providing a solid foundation for your own projects.

Step 3: Set Up a Virtual Environment and Install Dependencies

Creating a virtual environment helps isolate your project's dependencies. Run the following commands:

```bash
python -m venv mcp_env
source mcp_env/bin/activate  # On Windows use: mcp_env\Scripts\activate
pip install -r requirements.txt
```

This ensures that your MCP server has all the required libraries without affecting other projects.

Step 4: Run Your MCP Server Locally

With the environment set up, start your MCP server using:

```bash
python mcp_server.py
```

You should see output confirming that the server is running on your local machine. This is your testing ground for development and debugging.

Setting Up Cloud-Based MCP Development

Moving to a cloud-based environment enables you to simulate production conditions, manage scalability, and integrate with CI/CD pipelines. The following steps outline how to containerize your MCP server and deploy it to a cloud provider.

Step 1: Containerize Your MCP Server with Docker

First, create a `Dockerfile` in your MCP project directory:

```dockerfile
# Dockerfile
FROM python:3.9-slim

WORKDIR /app

 requirements.txt requirements.txt
RUN pip install --no-cache-dir -r requirements.txt

. .

EXPOSE 5000
CMD ["python", "mcp_server.py"]
```

Explanation:

- **Base Image:** We use a lightweight Python 3.9 image.
- **Working Directory:** The working directory is set to `/app`.
- **Dependencies:** The `requirements.txt` file is copied and installed.
- **Expose Port:** The container listens on port 5000.
- **Command:** The MCP server is started using the Python command.

Build the Docker image:

```bash
docker build -t mcp-server .
```

Step 2: Run Your Container Locally

Test your Docker container locally by running:

```bash
docker run -p 5000:5000 mcp-server
```

Your MCP server should now be accessible on `localhost:5000`, providing a reliable, reproducible environment that mirrors production.

Step 3: Deploy to a Cloud Provider

To deploy your container to a cloud service like AWS, GCP, or Azure, use their container orchestration services (e.g., AWS ECS, Google Kubernetes Engine, Azure Kubernetes Service). Here's a brief outline for deploying on Kubernetes:

1. **Create a Kubernetes Deployment File (deployment.yaml):**

```yaml
apiVersion: apps/v1
kind: Deployment
metadata:
  name: mcp-server-deployment
spec:
  replicas: 2
  selector:
    matchLabels:
      app: mcp-server
  template:
    metadata:
      labels:
        app: mcp-server
    spec:
      containers:
      - name: mcp-server
        image: mcp-server:latest
        ports:
        - containerPort: 5000
```

2. **Create a Service File (service.yaml):**

```yaml
apiVersion: v1
```

```
kind: Service
metadata:
  name: mcp-server-service
spec:
  selector:
    app: mcp-server
  ports:
    - protocol: TCP
      port: 80
      targetPort: 5000
  type: LoadBalancer
```

3. **Deploy to Kubernetes:**

```bash
kubectl apply -f deployment.yaml
kubectl apply -f service.yaml
```

These files define how your MCP server is deployed and exposed via a load balancer, making it accessible from the internet.

Essential Tools and Frameworks

Modern development relies on a robust toolchain to streamline workflows. Here are some essential tools and frameworks for MCP development:

- **IDE and Editors:** Visual Studio, PyCharm, or Sublime Text offer robust development features and extensions for Python and Node.js.
- **Version Control:** Git is indispensable for managing source and collaborating with teams.
- **Containerization:** Docker simplifies environment setup and deployment by encapsulating your application and its dependencies.
- **Orchestration:** Kubernetes is the leading tool for managing containerized applications in cloud environments.
- **MCP Frameworks:**
  - **FastMCP:** A TypeScript-based framework that accelerates MCP server development.
  - **MCP-Framework:** A Python toolkit designed to reduce boilerplate and standardize MCP tool integration.
- **CI/CD Pipelines:** Tools like Jenkins, GitHub Actions, or GitLab CI help automate testing and deployment processes.

Integrating these tools into your development environment ensures that your MCP projects are efficient, reproducible, and scalable. Whether you're running a local instance for quick iteration or deploying in the cloud for production, a solid toolchain is the foundation for success.

Commentary and Key Insights

My experience shows that investing in a well-organized development environment pays off in the long run. When I first transitioned from local development to containerized cloud deployments, the consistency and scalability of Docker and Kubernetes allowed my team to focus on innovation rather than troubleshooting environment inconsistencies. Adopting standardized frameworks like FastMCP or MCP-Framework further accelerates development by abstracting repetitive tasks and letting you concentrate on the unique logic of your application.

By integrating version control, containerization, and CI/CD pipelines into your workflow, you create a resilient, scalable, and maintainable development process. This integrated approach not only improves efficiency but also ensures that your MCP deployments can evolve with your business needs.

Conclusion

Setting up a robust development environment and leveraging the right toolchain are crucial steps for building scalable MCP-enabled systems. This guide has provided step-by-step instructions for both local and cloud-based development setups, from installing prerequisites to containerizing your application and deploying it with Kubernetes. Essential tools such as Docker, Git, and modern IDEs, alongside MCP-specific frameworks like FastMCP and MCP-Framework, form a powerful toolchain that streamlines development and deployment processes. With these practices in place, you can focus on building innovative, high-performance MCP integrations that are resilient, scalable, and ready for production.

7.2 Building, Testing, and Deploying MCP Servers

Building a robust MCP server is just the beginning; ensuring it performs reliably in production requires thorough testing and a well-defined deployment strategy. In this section, we cover the entire lifecycle—from building your MCP server to testing its functionality and finally deploying it in a production environment. The following guide includes detailed, step-by-step explanations along with complete, functional, and up-to-date examples.

Building the MCP Server

The first step is to build your MCP server. In our example, we'll use Python and Flask to create a simple JSON-RPC-based MCP server that exposes a tool (for instance, a basic "get_status" method). This server serves as a blueprint for how your AI agents will interact with external tools.

File: `mcp_server.py`

```python
#!/usr/bin/env python3
"""
A basic MCP server implemented using Flask that exposes a
'get_status' tool.
This server processes JSON-RPC requests and returns a
standardized response.
"""

from flask import Flask, request, jsonify
from datetime import datetime

app = Flask(__name__)

@app.route('/jsonrpc', methods=['POST'])
def jsonrpc():
    req = request.get_json()
    method = req.get("method")
    params = req.get("params", {})
    request_id = req.get("id")

    if method == "get_status":
        result = {
            "status": "running",
            "timestamp": datetime.utcnow().isoformat() + "Z"
```

```
        }
        response = {"jsonrpc": "2.0", "result": result, "id":
request_id}
    else:
        response = {
            "jsonrpc": "2.0",
            "error": {"code": -32601, "message": "Method not
found"},
            "id": request_id
        }

    return jsonify(response)

if __name__ == '__main__':
    # Run the server on localhost at port 5000
    app.run(host='127.0.0.1', port=5000)
```

Explanation:

- The Flask app creates a `/jsonrpc` endpoint that listens for POST requests.
- It processes the request by checking for the method `"get_status"` and returns a JSON-RPC compliant response including the server's status and current timestamp.
- If an unknown method is requested, it returns a standard error message.

Testing the MCP Server

Testing is crucial for ensuring that your MCP server behaves as expected. We can use Flask's built-in test client along with a testing framework like `pytest` to simulate JSON-RPC requests and verify responses.

File: `test_mcp_server.py`

```python
#!/usr/bin/env python3
"""
Tests for the MCP server using Flask's test client and
pytest.
"""

import json
```

```python
import pytest
from mcp_server import app

@pytest.fixture
def client():
    app.config['TESTING'] = True
    with app.test_client() as client:
        yield client

def test_get_status(client):
    # Build a JSON-RPC request payload for get_status
    payload = {
        "jsonrpc": "2.0",
        "method": "get_status",
        "params": {},
        "id": 1
    }
    response = client.post('/jsonrpc',
data=json.dumps(payload), content_type='application/json')
    data = json.loads(response.data)

    assert "result" in data
    assert data["result"]["status"] == "running"
    assert "timestamp" in data["result"]

def test_invalid_method(client):
    # Test a request with an invalid method
    payload = {
        "jsonrpc": "2.0",
        "method": "invalid_method",
        "params": {},
        "id": 2
    }
    response = client.post('/jsonrpc',
data=json.dumps(payload), content_type='application/json')
    data = json.loads(response.data)

    assert "error" in data
    assert data["error"]["code"] == -32601

if __name__ == '__main__':
    pytest.main()
```

Explanation:

- **Pytest Fixture:** The `client` fixture sets up the Flask test client for isolated testing.
- **Test Cases:** Two test cases are provided:

- o `test_get_status` sends a valid `get_status` request and checks that the response includes the expected status and timestamp.
- o `test_invalid_method` sends a request with an invalid method and verifies that the server returns an appropriate error.
- **Running Tests:** Execute the tests using `pytest` `test_mcp_server.py` to ensure your server meets the requirements.

Deploying the MCP Server

Once your MCP server is built and tested, the next step is deployment. Containerization with Docker is an effective way to ensure that your environment is consistent across development and production. Additionally, orchestration tools like Kubernetes can be used to manage your containers in a scalable cloud environment.

Step 1: Containerizing with Docker

Create a `Dockerfile` to containerize your MCP server.

File: `Dockerfile`

```dockerfile
dockerfile

# Use a lightweight Python image as the base image
FROM python:3.9-slim

# Set the working directory
WORKDIR /app

#  requirements and install dependencies
 requirements.txt .
RUN pip install --no-cache-dir -r requirements.txt

#  the MCP server into the container
 .  .

# Expose port 5000
EXPOSE 5000

# Define the command to run the MCP server
CMD ["python", "mcp_server.py"]
```

Explanation:

- **Base Image:** A slim version of Python 3.9 is used to keep the image lightweight.
- **Working Directory:** The project files are copied into `/app`.
- **Dependency Installation:** Dependencies listed in `requirements.txt` are installed.
- **Port Exposure and Command:** Port 5000 is exposed, and the server is started with `python mcp_server.py`.

Build the Docker image with:

```bash
docker build -t mcp-server .
```

Step 2: Running the Docker Container Locally

Test your Docker image by running a container:

```bash
docker run -p 5000:5000 mcp-server
```

Your MCP server should now be accessible on `localhost:5000`.

Step 3: Deploying to a Cloud Environment with Kubernetes

For production, you may deploy your Dockerized MCP server using Kubernetes. Below are sample deployment and service YAML files.

File: `deployment.yaml`

```yaml
apiVersion: apps/v1
kind: Deployment
metadata:
  name: mcp-server-deployment
spec:
  replicas: 2
  selector:
    matchLabels:
      app: mcp-server
  template:
```

```yaml
    metadata:
      labels:
        app: mcp-server
    spec:
      containers:
      - name: mcp-server
        image: mcp-server:latest
        ports:
        - containerPort: 5000
```

File: `service.yaml`

```yaml
yaml

apiVersion: v1
kind: Service
metadata:
  name: mcp-server-service
spec:
  selector:
    app: mcp-server
  ports:
    - protocol: TCP
      port: 80
      targetPort: 5000
  type: LoadBalancer
```

Explanation:

- **Deployment YAML:** Specifies that two replicas of your MCP server should be run, ensuring high availability.
- **Service YAML:** Exposes your deployment via a load balancer on port 80, forwarding requests to container port 5000.

Apply the configurations using:

```bash
bash

kubectl apply -f deployment.yaml
kubectl apply -f service.yaml
```

This deploys your MCP server to the Kubernetes cluster, making it accessible externally.

Commentary and Key Insights

Implementing a robust build, test, and deployment process is essential for any production system. Using Flask for your MCP server allows rapid development and testing locally, while containerization with Docker and orchestration with Kubernetes ensures that your deployment is scalable and reliable. In my experience, integrating automated testing into your development cycle significantly reduces bugs and downtime in production. The modular approach provided by MCP, combined with these modern toolchains, creates a resilient framework that can adapt to evolving business needs.

Conclusion

This section has guided you through the entire lifecycle of building, testing, and deploying MCP servers. We covered the creation of a basic MCP server using Flask, implemented comprehensive tests with Flask's test client and Pytest, and demonstrated containerization with Docker followed by deployment using Kubernetes. By following these detailed, step-by-step instructions and leveraging the provided examples, you can ensure that your MCP-enabled systems are robust, scalable, and ready for production. This thorough approach lays the foundation for developing and maintaining secure, high-performance AI integrations in any enterprise environment.

7.3 Overcoming Integration Challenges

Integrating MCP with diverse systems is powerful, but it's not without its challenges. When different components interact—each possibly built by different teams or even different vendors—issues such as data format mismatches, network latency, inconsistent protocols, and version incompatibilities can arise. In this section, we explore common pitfalls in MCP integration and outline practical strategies to overcome them. We provide detailed, step-by-step explanations and functional examples that demonstrate error handling, logging, retry mechanisms, and performance optimizations.

Common Integration Pitfalls

When deploying MCP in complex environments, several challenges often surface:

- **Data Format Inconsistencies:**
  Even with standardized protocols like JSON-RPC, slight variations in data structures can lead to parsing errors or unexpected behavior.
- **Network Latency and Connection Issues:**
  Communication between distributed systems can be affected by network delays, timeouts, or intermittent connectivity issues.
- **Error Handling and Retries:**
  Unforeseen errors—whether due to malformed requests, server overload, or external API failures—can disrupt operations if not managed properly.
- **Version Mismatches and Compatibility Issues:**
  As different tools and frameworks evolve, ensuring that all components remain compatible can be challenging.
- **Scalability Constraints:**
  Increased load might expose bottlenecks in the communication pipeline, affecting overall system performance.

Strategies for Robust Integration

A robust MCP integration strategy incorporates several key practices:

1. **Consistent Data Validation:**
   Ensure that all components strictly follow the JSON-RPC standard. Validate incoming and outgoing data to catch inconsistencies early.
2. **Comprehensive Error Handling:**
   Implement error-catching mechanisms that not only log errors but also gracefully recover from them. This includes retry logic for transient issues.
3. **Detailed Logging and Monitoring:**
   Use logging to trace request flows, monitor performance, and diagnose issues. Monitoring tools can provide real-time alerts when performance degrades.
4. **Retry and Timeout Mechanisms:**
   Build retry logic into your client applications to handle network

hiccups or temporary server issues, while also setting appropriate timeout values.

5. **Caching:**
   Implement caching for frequently requested data to reduce load and improve responsiveness, especially for data that does not change frequently.

6. **Modular and Version-Controlled Design:**
   Structure your system so that individual components can be updated or replaced without affecting the overall integration. Use version control to manage changes systematically.

Step-by-Step Implementation Example: Robust MCP Client

The following example demonstrates how to build a robust MCP client that communicates with an MCP server. The client includes error handling, logging, retry mechanisms, and basic caching to optimize performance.

Step 1: Set Up Logging and Configuration

Begin by configuring logging to capture detailed information for debugging and monitoring purposes.

File: `robust_mcp_client.py`

```python
#!/usr/bin/env python3
"""
A robust MCP client that demonstrates error handling,
logging, retries, and caching.
"""

import requests
import json
import time
import logging

# Configure logging
logging.basicConfig(level=logging.INFO, format="%(asctime)s
[%(levelname)s] %(message)s")

# Global cache for responses (simple in-memory caching)
response_cache = {}
```

```python
def call_mcp_method(url, method, params=None, request_id=1,
retries=3, timeout=5):
    """
    Sends a JSON-RPC request to the MCP server with error
handling and retries.

    Parameters:
        url (str): MCP server endpoint.
        method (str): The method to invoke.
        params (dict, optional): Parameters for the tool.
        request_id (int): Unique identifier for the request.
        retries (int): Number of retry attempts for transient
errors.
        timeout (int): Timeout for the HTTP request in
seconds.

    Returns:
        dict: The JSON-RPC response.
    """
    payload = {
        "jsonrpc": "2.0",
        "method": method,
        "params": params if params is not None else {},
        "id": request_id
    }
    headers = {"Content-Type": "application/json"}

    # Use caching for non-dynamic requests (example:
get_status might be cacheable)
    cache_key = f"{method}:{json.dumps(params,
sort_keys=True)}"
    if cache_key in response_cache:
        logging.info("Returning cached response for %s",
cache_key)
        return response_cache[cache_key]

    attempt = 0
    while attempt < retries:
        try:
            logging.info("Attempt %d: Calling MCP method
'%s'", attempt + 1, method)
            response = requests.post(url,
data=json.dumps(payload), headers=headers, timeout=timeout)
            response.raise_for_status()  # Raise HTTPError
for bad responses
            data = response.json()

            # Cache the response if applicable
            response_cache[cache_key] = data
            return data
```

114

```
        except requests.exceptions.RequestException as e:
            attempt += 1
            logging.error("Error calling MCP method '%s':
%s", method, e)
            time.sleep(2)   # Wait before retrying

    logging.error("Failed to call MCP method '%s' after %d
attempts", method, retries)
    return {"error": {"code": -32000, "message": "Failed to
call MCP method after retries"}, "id": request_id}

# Example usage
if __name__ == "__main__":
    server_url = "http://127.0.0.1:5000/jsonrpc"

    # Example: Call 'get_status' method on MCP server
    result = call_mcp_method(server_url, "get_status",
params={}, request_id=101)
    logging.info("get_status Response: %s",
json.dumps(result, indent=2))
```

Explanation:

- **Logging Configuration:** The logging is set up to capture INFO-level messages, providing timestamps and log levels.
- **Caching Mechanism:** A simple in-memory cache is implemented using a dictionary (`response_cache`) that stores responses keyed by method and parameters.
- **Error Handling and Retries:** The `call_mcp_method` function uses a while loop to attempt the request up to a specified number of retries. It logs errors and waits briefly between attempts.
- **Timeout Settings:** A timeout parameter ensures that the request does not hang indefinitely.
- **Usage Example:** The client attempts to call a `get_status` method on the MCP server, logging the response.

Step 2: Testing the Robust Client

Test the robust client with your MCP server running locally. This simulation demonstrates how the client handles connection issues, retries, and caches responses for efficiency. Modify the `server_url` as needed to match your deployment environment.

Commentary and Key Insights

Building a robust MCP client requires careful consideration of error handling and performance optimization. In my experience, integrating retries and caching mechanisms can significantly improve the reliability and responsiveness of a distributed system. By incorporating these strategies, you ensure that your AI agents receive consistent and timely responses, even in the face of transient network issues or server overloads.

The use of logging provides visibility into the system's behavior, making it easier to diagnose and resolve issues. These best practices are essential for maintaining a high-quality integration that can scale with increasing demands.

Conclusion

This section has provided a comprehensive guide to building, testing, and deploying MCP servers, with a focus on overcoming integration challenges. The robust MCP client example demonstrates how to implement error handling, logging, retries, and caching to create a resilient system. These strategies not only improve system reliability but also enhance performance and scalability. By following these detailed, step-by-step instructions and leveraging the provided examples, you can build an MCP integration that is robust, efficient, and ready for production environments. This approach sets the stage for developing complex, high-performance AI systems that are capable of seamless integration with diverse external tools and data sources.

Chapter 8: Future Trends and Innovations in Agentic AI

The landscape of artificial intelligence is evolving at an unprecedented pace, and agentic AI systems are at the forefront of this transformation. In this chapter, we explore the future trends and innovations shaping the development of autonomous AI agents. We discuss emerging research and technological advances, envision next-generation use cases, and analyze the anticipated enhancements in MCP standardization. Finally, we consider the societal, ethical, and economic impacts of these technologies and the preparations necessary for a future where human-AI collaboration is ubiquitous.

8.1 The Evolution of Agentic AI

Agentic AI has transformed from simple, rule-bound systems to complex, self-directed entities that can learn, collaborate, and adapt to their environments. This evolution is marked by a series of technological breakthroughs and research milestones that have gradually shifted the focus from mere automation to autonomous, intelligent behavior.

Early Beginnings: From Rules to Learning

In the early days of artificial intelligence, systems were primarily rule-based. These early AI models operated on a fixed set of instructions, much like a vending machine that dispenses a product when the correct button is pressed. While these systems could perform specific tasks with high reliability, they lacked the flexibility to adapt to new information or unforeseen situations. This rigidity meant that any change in the environment required a complete reprogramming of the system, limiting their utility in dynamic settings.

The introduction of machine learning marked the first major shift. Instead of relying solely on pre-defined rules, AI systems began to learn from data. Early machine learning models were designed to recognize patterns and make decisions based on statistical inferences. This allowed them to adapt to new data, albeit in a limited fashion. However, these systems still struggled with understanding context and maintaining coherent decision-making over extended interactions.

The Advent of Reinforcement Learning

A pivotal moment in the evolution of agentic AI came with the rise of reinforcement learning (RL). In RL, agents learn by interacting with their environment and receiving feedback in the form of rewards or penalties. This approach is akin to training a pet, where the animal learns the correct behavior through a system of rewards. Reinforcement learning enabled AI agents to develop strategies over time, optimizing their actions to achieve long-term goals.

The power of reinforcement learning became particularly evident in simulations and games, where agents could learn complex tasks such as navigating mazes, playing strategic board games, or even mastering video games. The success of RL in these environments demonstrated that AI agents could evolve from simple reactive systems to entities capable of planning, strategizing, and adapting based on their experiences.

Emergence of Multi-Agent Systems

As individual AI agents grew more capable, researchers began exploring the interactions among multiple agents. Multi-agent systems (MAS) introduced a new dimension of complexity—agents not only acted independently but also interacted with one another, sometimes cooperating and sometimes competing. These interactions led to emergent behaviors that were not explicitly programmed.

A classic example of this phenomenon is seen in virtual world simulations, such as those in Minecraft. Projects like the Sid Project have shown that when hundreds or even thousands of AI agents interact in a shared environment, complex social structures can emerge. Agents begin to specialize, forming roles similar to builders, traders, or administrators. Over time, these roles evolve into digital societies with their own economies, governance, and cultural norms. This emergence of collective behavior is a hallmark of agentic AI, demonstrating how simple interactions can scale into complex, dynamic systems.

Integration with Large Language Models and Contextual Understanding

The integration of large language models (LLMs) like GPT-4 and Claude has further accelerated the evolution of agentic AI. These models, which can understand and generate human-like text, provide AI agents with a deeper contextual understanding. They enable agents to interpret instructions, engage in complex dialogues, and make more nuanced decisions based on a wealth of contextual data.

By combining reinforcement learning with the capabilities of LLMs, agentic AI systems are now able to learn from both structured interactions and unstructured natural language inputs. This convergence allows agents to not only execute tasks but also to reason, reflect, and adapt their strategies over time. The result is a more robust, versatile form of AI that can operate in a variety of complex, real-world scenarios—from autonomous trading systems to intelligent personal assistants.

Personal Insights and Future Directions

Reflecting on the evolution of agentic AI, it's remarkable how far the field has come in a relatively short period. I remember when AI was predominantly about playing chess or solving simple puzzles; today, we are witnessing AI agents that can autonomously manage entire digital ecosystems, learn from human feedback, and even create new content. The journey from rigid, rule-based systems to adaptive, multi-agent environments illustrates not only technological progress but also the increasing complexity of the problems AI is expected to solve.

Looking ahead, the evolution of agentic AI is likely to continue at a rapid pace. We can anticipate further enhancements in how agents learn and interact, driven by ongoing research in deep reinforcement learning, neural-symbolic integration, and context-aware processing. Moreover, as AI systems become more integrated into daily life, their ability to collaborate with humans and other machines will be critical. This evolution will pave the way for more seamless, intuitive interactions that blur the lines between digital and physical worlds.

Conclusion

The evolution of agentic AI is a story of continuous innovation and adaptation. From early rule-based systems to the sophisticated, autonomous agents of today, each milestone has built upon the last to create systems that are more flexible, intelligent, and capable of complex interactions. Emerging research and technological advances are pushing the boundaries of what AI can do, while the integration of LLMs has enriched agents with deep contextual understanding. As we look to the future, the promise of agentic

AI lies in its ability to collaborate and adapt, transforming not only technology but the very way we interact with it.

8.2 The Future Role of MCP

The Model Context Protocol (MCP) is poised to become a foundational element in the evolution of intelligent systems, providing a standardized interface that simplifies the integration of AI models with an ever-expanding array of tools and data sources. As AI systems grow in complexity and capability, the role of MCP will evolve to meet the needs of increasingly interconnected and dynamic environments. This section explores how MCP is expected to enhance standardization and interoperability, and what a seamless AI ecosystem might look like in the near future.

Enhancements in Standardization and Interoperability

One of the key strengths of MCP is its ability to create a unified language for disparate systems. As more developers adopt MCP, we can expect significant enhancements that further standardize interactions across the board. Future iterations of MCP may incorporate dynamic schema evolution, allowing systems to adjust automatically as underlying data models change. This flexibility means that as new tools and technologies emerge, MCP can evolve without requiring a complete overhaul of existing integrations.

Standardization is not just about consistency—it's also about predictability. With a more refined MCP, every external tool or service that adheres to the protocol will deliver data in a consistent format. This predictability reduces the overhead associated with data parsing, error handling, and integration testing. Imagine an AI agent that can seamlessly switch between different data sources for real-time market analysis, healthcare diagnostics, or customer relationship management without needing custom connectors for each source. Enhanced standardization makes such seamless interoperability a practical reality.

Furthermore, as industries converge on MCP as the common integration protocol, collaborative efforts among developers will accelerate. Open-source communities and industry consortia are already working on improving various aspects of MCP, from security enhancements to performance optimizations. The result will be a more mature and robust standard that benefits everyone by reducing redundancy and lowering the barrier to entry for new integrations.

Predictions for a Seamless AI Ecosystem

Looking ahead, the future of AI integration is likely to be characterized by a highly interconnected ecosystem, where MCP plays a central role. In such an ecosystem, AI agents will be able to discover and leverage a vast array of MCP-compliant tools automatically. For example, an AI-driven personal assistant could, on the fly, determine the best available service for booking a flight, ordering groceries, or even scheduling meetings—without any manual configuration. This level of seamless integration will not only enhance user experience but also drive significant efficiency gains across industries.

Advancements in MCP could also lead to improved support for cross-platform integration. As AI models and external systems continue to evolve, a unified protocol like MCP will ensure that switching between platforms—whether from on-premise to cloud-based systems or between different cloud providers—is smooth and hassle-free. The ability to operate in a heterogeneous environment without compromising on performance or security is a game-changer for enterprises looking to future-proof their IT infrastructures.

Moreover, as MCP becomes more widely adopted, we can expect it to serve as the backbone for next-generation AI applications that operate in real time and at scale. Imagine smart cities where every sensor, device, and digital service communicates through a standardized MCP layer, enabling autonomous decision-making that optimizes urban infrastructure and public services. Similarly, in the financial sector, MCP-enabled trading systems could integrate real-time data feeds, execute complex trading strategies, and manage risk across multiple markets—all through a single, standardized interface.

Expert Commentary and Personal Insights

From my perspective, the evolution of MCP reflects a broader trend in technology toward standardization and modularity. In the early days of integration, custom-built connectors were the norm, leading to silos and inefficiencies. With MCP, we see a clear shift towards a more open, collaborative approach that leverages community input to refine and improve the standard continuously.

I have witnessed firsthand how standardization in other domains—like the universal USB-C connector in consumer electronics—can drive innovation and simplify user experiences. As MCP matures, I expect it to have a similar transformative effect on AI integrations. The ability to plug any AI agent into a rich ecosystem of tools without bespoke development is a powerful enabler for rapid innovation.

Conclusion

The future role of MCP is set to be transformative. Enhancements in standardization and interoperability will enable a seamless AI ecosystem where agents can dynamically discover, access, and integrate external tools with minimal friction. This evolution will facilitate the development of intelligent systems that are not only more efficient and secure but also adaptable to the rapid pace of technological change.

By establishing MCP as the universal protocol for AI tool integration, we lay the groundwork for a future where digital services are interconnected, scalable, and responsive to real-time needs. As the technology matures, both developers and end-users will benefit from a more cohesive and efficient environment, driving innovations that were once only imaginable.

8.3 Societal, Ethical, and Economic Impacts

Autonomous AI systems, powered by technologies like MCP, are reshaping our society in profound ways. Their influence extends beyond technical innovation—these systems affect how we work, communicate, and even govern ourselves. In this section, we explore the broader societal, ethical, and economic implications of widespread AI integration, focusing on both the opportunities and the challenges that lie ahead.

Societal Impacts

Autonomous AI systems have the potential to transform everyday life. As AI agents become more capable of performing complex tasks—from managing urban infrastructure to providing personalized healthcare—they can significantly enhance efficiency and convenience. For example, in smart cities, AI-driven systems can optimize traffic flow, reduce energy consumption, and improve public safety by coordinating data from multiple sources in real time. This integration can lead to higher living standards and more resilient communities.

However, the societal impact of AI is a double-edged sword. While these systems can improve productivity and quality of life, they also raise concerns about job displacement and the digital divide. Automation may replace routine, manual tasks, potentially leading to unemployment in certain sectors. At the same time, the benefits of AI may be unevenly distributed, with those who have access to advanced technologies reaping significant rewards while others are left behind. Addressing these disparities will require proactive measures in education, retraining, and policy-making to ensure that the transformative potential of AI benefits all segments of society.

Ethical Considerations

The ethical dimensions of agentic AI systems are multifaceted. One primary concern is transparency. As AI agents make decisions autonomously, it becomes crucial to understand the rationale behind their actions. Without transparency, there is a risk that these systems may inadvertently reinforce biases or make decisions that are difficult to justify. Efforts in explainable AI are essential to ensure that decision-making processes are clear and that accountability is maintained.

Another ethical issue is privacy. AI systems often rely on large datasets, some of which contain sensitive personal information. Balancing the need for data to improve AI performance with the imperative to protect individual privacy is a significant challenge. This balance can be achieved through techniques such as data anonymization, secure data storage, and strict access controls, all of which must be integrated into the design of AI systems from the ground up.

Furthermore, there is the question of agency and autonomy. As AI agents become more independent, determining responsibility for their actions becomes complex. If an AI system makes a decision that leads to unintended consequences, who is accountable—the developer, the user, or the system itself? Establishing ethical guidelines and regulatory frameworks is critical to navigate these challenges and ensure that AI development aligns with broader societal values.

Economic Impacts

The economic ramifications of agentic AI systems are substantial. On one hand, AI has the potential to drive significant economic growth by increasing productivity, optimizing supply chains, and reducing operational costs across industries. For instance, in finance, AI trading agents can analyze massive datasets in real time and execute trades with remarkable speed and precision. In manufacturing, AI-driven automation can streamline production processes, reduce waste, and improve product quality. These advancements can lead to higher profit margins and a competitive edge for businesses that adopt AI technologies.

On the other hand, the economic impact is not uniformly positive. The rapid pace of automation raises concerns about job displacement, particularly in sectors that rely heavily on routine tasks. The transition to an AI-driven economy may result in significant shifts in the labor market, necessitating robust strategies for workforce retraining and social support. Additionally, economic gains from AI may concentrate in the hands of a few large corporations that can afford to invest in cutting-edge technologies, potentially exacerbating income inequality.

The challenge, therefore, lies in harnessing the economic benefits of AI while mitigating the risks of unemployment and inequality. This requires a combination of forward-thinking policies, investment in education and reskilling programs, and a commitment to ensuring that the economic rewards of AI are broadly shared across society.

Preparing for a Future of Human-AI Collaboration

The transition to a world where autonomous AI systems play a significant role is not just a technical challenge—it is a societal one. To prepare for this future, organizations and governments need to establish comprehensive strategies that address ethical, social, and economic concerns. This includes:

- **Regulatory Frameworks:** Developing policies that ensure transparency, accountability, and fairness in AI decision-making processes.
- **Education and Training:** Investing in education and workforce training programs to help individuals adapt to an AI-driven economy.
- **Public-Private Partnerships:** Encouraging collaboration between governments, industry, and academia to promote research and share best practices in AI development and ethics.

- **Inclusive Design:** Ensuring that AI systems are designed to be accessible and beneficial to all, minimizing the risk of exacerbating existing social and economic inequalities.

Conclusion

The evolution of agentic AI, underpinned by standards like MCP, is not merely a technical achievement—it represents a transformative shift with far-reaching societal, ethical, and economic implications. As these systems become more autonomous and integrated into our daily lives, it is essential to address the challenges of transparency, privacy, and accountability, while also harnessing their potential to drive economic growth and improve quality of life.

By establishing robust ethical guidelines, investing in education and workforce development, and implementing forward-thinking policies, we can ensure that the rise of autonomous AI systems benefits society as a whole. This balanced approach will pave the way for a future where human-AI collaboration is both productive and equitable, fostering an environment where technology enhances our lives without compromising our values.

Conclusion

This book has taken you on a journey through the evolving landscape of agentic AI integration, highlighting the transformative potential of the Model Context Protocol (MCP) in enabling seamless, scalable, and secure interactions between intelligent systems and external tools. We explored the evolution of AI agents from simple rule-based systems to complex, autonomous entities capable of emergent behavior. Along the way, you learned how MCP standardizes tool integration, how to wrap and expose functionalities as callable MCP tools, and how to build, test, and deploy robust MCP servers.

Recap of Key Insights

- **Evolution of Agentic AI:**
  We began by examining the progression from early, rule-bound AI to sophisticated agents capable of learning, collaboration, and adaptive decision-making. This evolution has paved the way for systems that not only perform tasks but also interact dynamically within complex environments.
- **The Role of MCP:**
  MCP emerged as the universal language that bridges AI models with a variety of external tools. Its standardized architecture—comprising hosts, clients, and servers—ensures consistent, secure, and efficient communication. This has dramatically reduced the need for custom-built connectors, streamlining integration across disparate systems.
- **Practical Integration and Customization:**
  We demonstrated how to convert existing functions into MCP tools and expose them through a standard protocol. Customization of these tools allows organizations to tailor integrations to their specific business needs, whether it's optimizing workflows in enterprise settings or enhancing the emergent behavior of AI agents in virtual worlds.
- **Security and Privacy:**
  Robust security measures, including encryption, token-based authentication, and role-based access control, are essential for protecting sensitive data in MCP deployments. Effective risk assessment and mitigation strategies further ensure the integrity and reliability of your systems.
- **Real-World Applications:**
  The practical case studies on gaming, financial trading, and enterprise

automation illustrated the diverse applications of MCP. These examples showed how standardized integration can drive innovation and efficiency across various industries.

- **Future Trends:**
Looking ahead, advancements in AI, combined with continuous enhancements in MCP, promise a future where intelligent systems are more interconnected and context-aware. This will foster a seamless AI ecosystem that benefits businesses, individuals, and society at large.

Vision for the Future of Agentic AI Integration

The future of agentic AI integration is one of boundless potential. We envision a world where AI agents, empowered by MCP, can interact seamlessly with every facet of our digital and physical environments. Imagine smart cities where AI orchestrates urban infrastructure, autonomous financial systems that react instantaneously to market changes, and enterprise environments where data flows effortlessly between systems, driving innovation and operational excellence.

Standardization will not only accelerate the adoption of new technologies but also ensure that these systems remain secure, scalable, and interoperable. As research and development in areas like reinforcement learning, explainable AI, and natural language processing continue to advance, the capabilities of AI agents will expand, making them indispensable partners in both our professional and personal lives.

Final Thoughts and Call to Action

The integration of agentic AI and MCP is more than just a technological advancement—it's a paradigm shift that will reshape industries and transform our daily lives. By embracing these innovations, developers and organizations have the opportunity to build systems that are smarter, more adaptive, and capable of driving significant economic and social change.

I encourage you to take the insights and practical strategies presented in this book and apply them to your own projects. Experiment with MCP, customize your integrations, and contribute to the evolving ecosystem of agentic AI. Whether you're an experienced developer or new to the field, your work in this area has the potential to make a lasting impact.

The future is being built today. Join the movement, innovate boldly, and help create a world where intelligent systems enhance our capabilities and improve our quality of life.

Appendices

A. Glossary of Terms and Concepts

Agentic AI:
Intelligent systems designed to operate autonomously by learning, adapting, and making decisions without continuous human intervention. These agents can interact with their environments, collaborate with other agents, and evolve over time to meet specific objectives.

AI Agent:
A software program that utilizes artificial intelligence techniques to perform tasks, make decisions, and interact with data and tools. AI agents can be task-specific or general-purpose and are often designed to operate in complex, dynamic environments.

JSON-RPC:
A lightweight remote procedure call protocol that uses JSON (JavaScript Object Notation) to encode messages. JSON-RPC enables standardized communication between clients and servers, making it a critical component in MCP for ensuring uniform data exchange.

MCP (Model Context Protocol):
A standardized protocol that bridges AI models with external tools and data sources. MCP provides a uniform interface, typically based on JSON-RPC, to facilitate seamless integration, secure communication, and interoperability among various systems.

MCP Host:
An AI agent or application that initiates requests and utilizes external functionalities provided through the MCP ecosystem. The host is responsible for sending JSON-RPC requests and processing responses received from MCP servers.

MCP Client:
The component that acts as an intermediary between the MCP host and the MCP server. It manages communication by formatting requests according to the MCP standard and routing responses back to the host.

MCP Server:
A service or application that exposes specific functionalities or data sources

via the MCP protocol. MCP servers handle incoming JSON-RPC requests, perform the necessary actions or data retrieval, and return standardized responses to the client.

Decorator (in Python):
A design pattern in Python used to modify or extend the behavior of a function or method. In the context of MCP tools, a decorator is used to register functions as callable tools by adding them to a global registry.

Tool Registry:
A centralized collection or dictionary that stores functions registered as MCP tools. The registry allows MCP servers to dynamically look up and execute functions based on the method name specified in a JSON-RPC request.

Role-Based Access Control (RBAC):
A security strategy that restricts system access based on the roles assigned to users or components. In MCP deployments, RBAC ensures that only authorized agents can access sensitive data or functionalities.

Token-Based Authentication:
A security mechanism in which users or systems must provide a valid token (e.g., an API key or JWT) to access resources. This method is used in MCP deployments to verify the identity of clients and ensure that only authorized requests are processed.

Reinforcement Learning (RL):
A machine learning paradigm where an agent learns to make decisions by interacting with an environment and receiving rewards or penalties. RL is a key technology behind the evolution of agentic AI, enabling agents to optimize their behavior through trial and error.

Emergent Behavior:
Complex and unexpected patterns or behaviors that arise from the interaction of simpler components. In the context of agentic AI, emergent behavior refers to the sophisticated social structures and dynamics that can develop when multiple AI agents interact under standardized protocols.

Multi-Agent Systems (MAS):
Systems composed of multiple interacting AI agents that collaborate, compete, or operate independently within a shared environment. MAS are central to studies of emergent behavior and complex decision-making in AI.

Standardization:
The process of establishing and implementing technical standards to ensure consistency and compatibility across systems. MCP standardization enables uniform data exchange and reduces integration complexity across diverse platforms.

Interoperability:
The ability of different systems, devices, or software to work together seamlessly. In MCP, interoperability is achieved by adhering to a common protocol, allowing AI agents to access a variety of external tools and data sources without custom integration efforts.

Containerization:
A lightweight virtualization technique that encapsulates an application and its dependencies in a container. Tools like Docker are used to ensure that MCP servers run in consistent environments across development and production.

Orchestration:
The automated management, deployment, and scaling of containerized applications, typically using platforms such as Kubernetes. Orchestration enables MCP deployments to scale efficiently and maintain high availability in cloud environments.

CI/CD (Continuous Integration/Continuous Deployment):
A set of practices and tools that automate the process of integrating changes, testing, and deploying applications. CI/CD pipelines help maintain the reliability and consistency of MCP deployments by ensuring that any changes are thoroughly tested before being rolled out.

B. Sample Repositories and Tutorials

Official MCP Repositories:

- **Model Context Protocol Servers:**
  A comprehensive repository featuring reference implementations of MCP servers for various use cases. This repository includes both Python and Node.js examples, detailed documentation, and guidelines for extending MCP functionalities.

- GitHub URL:
  https://github.com/modelcontextprotocol/servers
- **Awesome MCP Servers:**
  A curated list of MCP server projects contributed by the community. This resource aggregates production-ready servers, experimental projects, and tools that follow the MCP standard, offering a one-stop reference for developers.
  - GitHub URL: Awesome MCP Servers Repository

Frameworks and Toolkits:

- **FastMCP:**
  A TypeScript-based framework designed to streamline the development of MCP servers. FastMCP offers pre-built modules, configuration templates, and integration utilities that reduce development time and ensure consistency.
  - GitHub URL: FastMCP Repository *(Replace with actual URL if available)*
- **MCP-Framework:**
  A Python toolkit aimed at minimizing boilerplate for MCP integration. This framework provides utilities for building, testing, and deploying MCP servers, along with examples and tutorials.
  - GitHub URL: MCP-Framework Repository *(Replace with actual URL if available)*

Tutorials and Learning Resources:

- **Building an AI Agent with MCP and LangChain Adapters:**
  A detailed tutorial that demonstrates how to integrate MCP with AI agents using LangChain adapters. This resource covers setting up the environment, registering tools, and deploying an MCP server, with step-by-step examples.
  - URL: Building an AI Agent with MCP and LangChain Adapters
- **Introduction to JSON-RPC for MCP:**
  An educational resource that explains the basics of JSON-RPC, its role in MCP, and best practices for formatting requests and responses. This tutorial is ideal for developers new to the protocol.
  - URL: *(Search for "Introduction to JSON-RPC for MCP" on relevant platforms)*
- **Docker and Kubernetes for MCP Deployment:**
  A tutorial that walks you through containerizing your MCP server

with Docker and deploying it on a Kubernetes cluster. This guide covers creating Dockerfiles, building images, and writing Kubernetes deployment files.

- o URL: *(Search for "Docker Kubernetes MCP Deployment Tutorial" on relevant platforms)*
- **CI/CD Pipelines for MCP Integrations:**
  A step-by-step guide on setting up continuous integration and continuous deployment pipelines for MCP projects. This tutorial highlights best practices for automating tests, deployments, and monitoring.
  - o URL: *(Search for "CI/CD MCP Integration Tutorial" on relevant platforms)*

These repositories and tutorials provide a solid foundation for building, testing, and deploying MCP-enabled systems. They offer practical, implementable examples and detailed documentation that will help you navigate the challenges of integrating AI agents with external tools using the Model Context Protocol. Whether you are a beginner or an experienced developer, these resources are invaluable for mastering MCP and harnessing its full potential in your projects.

www.ingramcontent.com/pod-product-compliance
Lightning Source LLC
LaVergne TN
LVHW080117070326
832902LV00015B/2643